While every precaution has been taken in the preparation of this book, the publisher assumes no responsibility for errors or omissions, or for damages resulting from the use of the information contained herein.

BEIJING AND BEYOND: EATING (AND SPENDING) OUR WAY THROUGH CHINA, WITH PERSONAL REFLECTIONS ON CHINA'S COMING-OF-AGE CRIMINAL JUSTICE SYSTEM... AND OF MY FELLOW TRAVELERS, 1981

First edition. October 29, 2014.

Copyright © 2014 Michael A. Kroll.

ISBN: 979-8224691203

Written by Michael A. Kroll.

Beijing & Beyond:
Eating (and spending) our way through China with personal reflections on China's coming of age criminal justice system … and of my fellow travelers, 1981

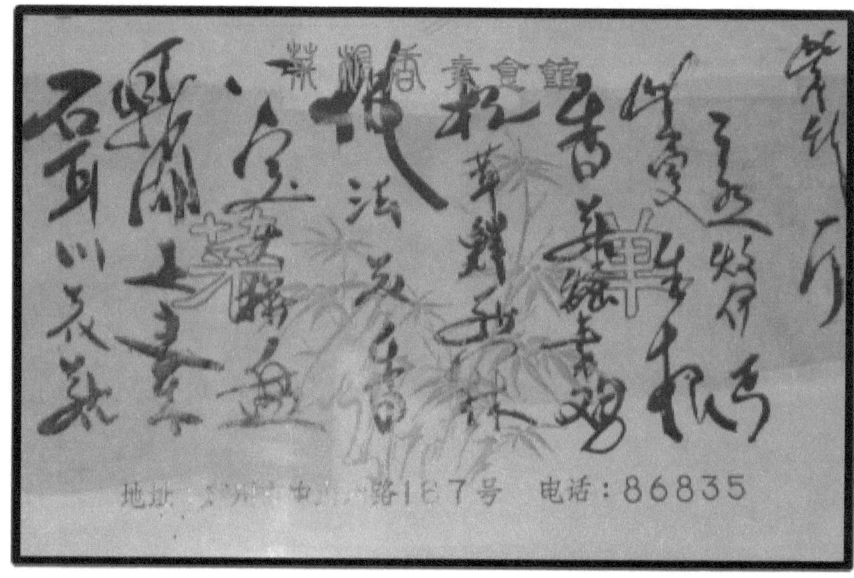

By Michael A. Kroll
Smashwords Edition
Copyright 2014 Michael A. Kroll
Smashwords Edition License Notes

Thank you for respecting the hard work of this author.
Website: http://www.michael-a-kroll.com/
Email: michaelkroll@michaelwrites.org

Beijing and Beyond

Eating (and spending) our way through China with personal reflections on China's coming of age criminal justice system ... and of my fellow travelers, 1981

List of Photographs

62. Kay Harris, friend and fellow traveler, Hanauma Bay, Hawaii

Preface

In May of 1981, I was given an incredible opportunity to visit China. I was then the Coordinator of the NMPC, the National Moratorium on Prison Construction, in Washington, D.C. (Funded by the Unitarian Universalist Service Committee, we had staff in Atlanta, Chicago, San Francisco and, of course, D.C.) My counterpart in San Francisco, Naneen Karraker, had just inherited some money, and asked if I'd be interested in joining a People-to-People criminal justice tour of that once-forbidden country. Because she was pregnant at the time, she decided it was prudent to remain here, but wanted to see, through my eyes, what "criminal justice" looked like in a country that had been closed to the outside world — and especially to the United States — since Mao Tse Tung's Communist victory over the Nationalists in 1949. Only a decade before had Americans been provided their first glimpse into China, when, in April of 1971, an American ping-pong team was permitted entry, and the world was introduced to Ping-Pong diplomacy, negotiated by President Nixon's Secretary of State, Henry Kissinger.

In January of 1981, less than six months before we began our journey, Mao's widow, Jiang Qing and the Gang of Four, had been convicted of "anti-party activities" and sentenced to death. Mao Tse Tung had died only three years earlier, in 1978, and was replaced by Deng Xiaoping as China's preeminent leader. It was a time of transformation in China. There was no air pollution. There were barely any cars. Urban renewal had only just begun. And university students — who were born shortly after Mao launched his disastrous "Cultural Revolution" that had victimized so many of their parents — saw an opportunity to influence the changes that were coming. Like students everywhere, they were impatient for promised reforms and reforms they wished to be promised. Their impatience was met with a brutal military assault on thousands of student reformers massed in

Tiananmen Square in 1989, just eight years after we were to get our own brief glimpse of China in transition. The tour would be led by Diana (Dinni) Gordon, the director of the progressive National Council on Crime and Delinquency. I didn't hesitate a second before accepting Naneen's generous offer.

The only person I knew that would be on this tour was my predecessor at the NMPC, Kay Harris, who was then just beginning her tenure as a criminal justice professor at Temple University in Philadelphia. She and I were very good friends, which made the prospect of this tour even more appealing.

During the trip, I kept a daily log, which is the basis for what follows.

....

In addition to my gratitude to Naneen Karraker for making this trip possible (and to the Unitarian Universalist Service Committee who permitted me to make this journey while in their employ), I am also indebted to the memoirists with whom I meet every week to share our work. They sat patiently, week after week, hearing me read, and offering me their wise and always encouraging comments, some praiseworthy, some critical, but all of it making this a much stronger narrative.

Thank you, Jimmy, for putting up with me.

Cover art: Hand-drawn menu from vegetarian restaurant, Guangzhou (Canton)

May 28, 1981 — Narita, Japan

Ohiyo gozaimasu! It has been nearly eight years since I taught English here in Japan. The sense of unreality about being back is completely overshadowed by the fantasy that I am about to embark on, however. I am on my way to China! Behind me lies my decision to leave the Moratorium office in Washington, and return to California (though I have not yet divulged this decision to the UU Service Committee, which controls my purse strings.) With this decision comes both the immense relief of having made a choice, and the vague anxiety of facing an unknown future. But for the moment, the disturbing past and the uncertain future can be set aside, banished as much as possible from the conscious present.

And speaking of the present, a box of "presents" from UUSC headquarters in Boston was waiting for me at the Sea-Tac Airport when we arrived in Seattle. It contained dozens of the Service Committee's latest promotional gimmick — a green plastic visor with the words "Unitarian Universalist Service Committee" inscribed over an image of their logo, the eternal flame. Along with it came a telegram telling me to hand these out as gifts while traveling through China. For the first time, I examined the visors closely, then took far too much pleasure in composing my own telegram back to headquarters: "Would love to hand out these visors for you, but the damn things are made in Taiwan!" I can only imagine their relief when they get my resignation letter next month.

Anyway, unlike the rest of the group, which met in Seattle yesterday for the People-to-People orientation (orienting us to the Orient), Kay and I were spared. At the time, we were attending the National Jail Coalition meeting in Minnesota, after which we flew to Seattle where the official trip begins, meeting our fellow travelers at the airport shortly before boarding the plane that would take us to Asia.

Judging from their comments, Orientation was a day and a half of sexist jokes, coupled with what passes for the wise advice of the experienced traveler. "Don't eat except in approved restaurants. Don't wander away from the group." It's the same sort of "advice" that I heard fifteen years ago as an eager Peace Corps volunteer about to begin three years of English teaching in Borneo. The only difference is that I believed it then.

There are 31 people in this tour, including a couple of older Federal judges, several state and city prison administrators, an associate prison warden, an assistant D.A., someone in the Justice Department, and a number of criminal justice research people and advocates — mostly young lawyer types. There are two black people, one being an ex-prisoner who runs an organization, which markets prison art. He spent 19 years in our finest facilities. Ironically, the only other African American is an assistant prison warden. There are assorted wives (who are described in the official People-to-People Delegate Biographies as "Wife of ___) And, of course, there is Kay and me. Thirty criminal justice professionals and one anti-professional...

Oh, yes. There is also one person whom I am really looking forward to meeting and spending time with. He is listed as "Justice Editor" for Newsweek Magazine, which makes him, for me, the one "star" among us. As our Northwest Orient 747 carried us across the Pacific, I played the game of trying to determine which delegate he was. Of course, I was able to eliminate the few who always make a point of pumping hands and introducing themselves, like the stereotypical American tourist with multiple cameras slung over his shoulder, an actor's smile, which never leaves his lips, except when engaged in animated conversation (never any other kind). He represents the Polaroid Company, which apparently has an exemplary employment program for ex-prisoners, and, to be fair, despite his recognizable type, I like him.

The person I've decided must be Aric, the journalist, is a young man wearing glasses and tan pants and sitting on the other side of the plane from me. I picked him because I didn't see him utter a single word during the entire nine-hour flight.

We arrived last evening at the Narita International Airport — the one which the local farmers so bitterly opposed building a decade ago. The symbols of that bitter controversy are everywhere present: hundreds of armed soldiers and miles of Razor Ribbon-topped fencing surround the airport. In fact, the perimeter security resembles nothing more than a prison — an appropriate reception for this group.

I suppose as punishment for missing Orientation, Kay and I have both been stricken with mini-tragedies.

Hers occurred in flight. When she got her luggage at the airport, she discovered that an oily perfume — not hers — had permeated her cloth bag, staining much of what she had packed. She was subjected to the endless Japanese bureaucratic form-filling, an absolute necessity if she wants to recover her losses, while the group waited impatiently on the two small buses that would take us through the military zone surrounding the airport to the hotel.

The hotel was my mini-tragedy. We are staying in a "modern" American-type place, a cross between a Howard Johnson's and a Motel 6. I have been anticipating my one night in Japan after so long an absence, soaking in a deep hot tub, sampling the sushi bar, walking barefoot or with *tabi* in my hotel room. Well, there is no Japanese *ofuro* bath, no Japanese food, no *tatami* mat floors. We had tasteless veal cutlets for dinner. One need never know one has left the United States. What a grave disappointment! Granted, my disappointment does not rise to the level of Kay's loss, and — with the thought of this afternoon's departure keenly in mind, and the fact that the real Japan is just outside the hotel — I am bearing up fairly well, deprived as I am.

I am sitting on a rock by the edge of a beautiful Japanese pond. It is in the middle of Narita Fudo, one of the most famous of Japanese temples. I am spending perhaps the last half-day of solitude possible for the next three weeks. I took the city bus (100 yen) here this morning from the hotel. The greatest number of our group, perhaps 20 of them, have rented their own tour bus in order to spend half a day in Tokyo, about an hour and a half away. The remaining ten are either going into Tokyo on their own or going as a group into Narita. I demurred. I kipped Tokyo because I have been there before, and because one can't possible appreciate the excitement of that city in a four-hour morning tour in the company of 20 other Americans. I resisted joining the smaller group excursions because I know that being alone will become increasingly difficult from today onward. I also know that my craving for solitude will grow in direct proportion to its unattainability.

Fudu Temple, Narita, Japan

The village of Narita itself makes up for the hotel. It is like a thousand other villages in Japan: narrow shop-lined streets, pulsing with pedestrian traffic under overhanging neon signs, which seem to scream their messages at you in huge characters representing all three of Japan's alphabets, *Katakana, Hiragana* and *Kanji*. My favorite shop was one where four Japanese men, each wearing a white head-band, were picking out live, wriggling eels from a huge vat, securing them on a cutting board by pushing their heads down over a nail, and then slitting them up the side. I shuddered as I watched, which obviously amused them (the men, not the eels), but I must confess that *unagi* is one of my favorite Japanese dishes, so I squelched my squeamishness. And, when you stop to think about it, a beef slaughterhouse is much gorier.

The temple is huge, filled with Japanese-roofed pagodas and Shinto shrines with crowds of Japanese — mostly women, and mostly older — bowing and clapping their hands, and making special appeals to the appropriate *kami-samas*, their Shinto gods. As I sit and write this from one side of a large pond, I can see a group of Japanese boys, dressed in red uniforms, and girls, dressed in blue, making their way around the opposite shore. Leading this group of high school students is a teacher with a flag that all can see and rally around — the same as Japanese tour groups everywhere.

Japanese women bowing in prayer at Fudu Temple, Narita, Japan I have not had my fill of being alone in this place yet, and I don't think I'm ready for the adventure, which begins in earnest, a few short hours from now. But it is getting late, and I must soon catch the bus back to the hotel. Carrying my shoulder bag filled with camera and film, writing pad and pen, and novel (<u>China Men</u>, by Maxine Hong Kingston), I will make my way back through the immense grounds of Fudo-san, and treat myself to a sushi lunch somewhere. The hotel lunch is paid for, of course, but I don't want the taste of hamburger in my mouth as I board the plane for Beijing.

May 28, En route to Beijing

It seems utterly unbelievable, but "this plane is bound for China, this plane." The blue Pan Am baggage claim stub they stapled to my ticket back in Minneapolis says, unambiguously, "Peking". I don't know whether Pan Am just hasn't gotten around to changing their forms from the old spelling to the new — Beijing — or whether they are stubbornly refusing to give in to the audacity of a government trying to free itself from the colonial influences that remain, like the American sports announcers who stubbornly refused to acknowledge the transition of Cassius Clay to Mohammed Ali.

What looms immediately ahead is a three-week trip into China, a mere glimpse into the great, formerly forbidden Middle Kingdom, the People's Republic. We will see Ministers of Justice and Peoples' Courts, law schools and lawyers' committees, reform schools and prisons. We will travel to Beijing, Nanjing (formerly Nanking) — where I will pass my 38th birthday — Wuxi, Suzhou, Shanghai and Guangzhou (Canton) before exiting through Hong Kong. It is, in many ways, the realization of a long-nourished fantasy.

At the same time, though, my "mental state" is precarious. The relationship between me and UUSC headquarters in Boston is strained to the breaking point. Indeed, I had to wage a quietly furious battle to convince them, reluctantly and jealously, to consider this trip work-related. To make sure this doesn't qualify as "vacation time," they imposed a requirement that I submit a written report upon returning to my Washington office, as if I don't routinely submit written reports to the Board of my professional activities, something that I've always considered a regular part of the job. The boss also made clear, before my departure, that I was "to wear my UUSC hat at all times" — presumably that tacky green visor made in Taiwan.

The most infuriating part of their continual reminders of our employer-employee relationship is the fact that this trip is being financed entirely without their help. I have to admit that it is not coming out of my pocket, either, but that is only because the $4,000 price tag would have put it well beyond my reach. As you know, I have a fairy godmother to back me on this trip. My "rich" friend had just come into a small inheritance, which she was looking to donate to a tax-deductible charity, when I inveigled her to donate it to the UUSC, earmarked for my criminal justice China tour. Because a private foundation has an agreement with the UUSC to match any contribution of $50 or more, they are now $4,000 richer than they were, even after forking over my dough. But instead of being grateful for that, their tone and attitude suggests that I am somehow taking advantage of them without the requisite institutional loyalty.

Historically, I seek the solace of solitude at times like these, but that solace is not possible here. I thank god for Kay who, with her gregarious personality and knowledge of all aspects of criminal justice, is my bridge to the others. It's also true that the anthropologist/ sociologist in me is intrigued by this group of Americans, so much like other groups of American tourists in some ways — rich and open, eager to be liked — and so unlike other American tourists in other ways — in their concern for social justice, for example, if nothing else.

Beyond that, some among this group would be intriguing in any situation: a Boston prosecutor named Pebble who looks and sounds like Jacqueline Kennedy; a middle-aged one-armed attorney who served as counsel to the Peace Corps in its formative years; an immaculately-dressed, perfectly coiffed woman named Pearl, who directs the California Youth Authority, California's prison system for children; a nineteen-year veteran of the American penal system who is the most affable, ebullient, and hilarious person present (so far); a strange couple who dress in identical outfits and whose names I don't know yet since they've said nothing to anybody; and a Harvard graduate lawyer who's never practiced law leading the group.

I was right about the bespectacled young man on the opposite side of the plane from me. He is Aric Press of Newsweek, who, I am happy to report after my first conversation with him, will certainly be a friend.

In short, despite my general misgivings about group travel, there are some interesting people here. I have no doubt that in our three weeks of constant companionship, I will form, unform, and reform a million perceptions about my fellow travelers. I hope I will be able to capture at least some of my evolving perceptions as we embark on this incredible journey.

I hope, too, that I can submerge my claustrophobic, anti-social tendencies for the trip's duration, until I emerge — with Kay — into the Honolulu sun for two days of R&R on the way back through California to D.C. where my work awaits me.

May 28, Beijing: Arrival

Can it be that I am writing this from China? Is it possible that a dream of a lifetime can suddenly become reality after a short, two-hour flight? My sense of unreality is aggravated by the lateness of the hour (after midnight) and the length of the day, which began very early in Narita. But unreality is the only word I can think of that describes my feelings.

I am sitting at the desk in our room at the State Guest House (Villa #11). I say "our" room because we have each been assigned a roommate for the duration of the trip. Mine is Doug McDonald, a sociologist from the Vera Institute, which does some of the most reliable and respected criminal justice research in the country. He's about my age and has spent some time himself in prison for selling dope to an undercover agent (those scummy leeches), and I think he's a good choice for a roommate.

Villa #11, State Guest House (Daioyutai)

We were met at the airport by our tour guide, Mr. Wong, who will remain with us for the entire trip, though we will also have local guides in each city we visit. Beijing is Mr. Wong's city, and here he will be our only guide. He is a good-looking man who appears to be about 25 years old, and is probably a decade or more older. His running commentary on the bus trip from the airport was wonderfully charming. "You'll find soft drinks, beer and juice in the refrigerator that is in each of your rooms. Please drink as much as you can. Peking" (yes, he said Peking) "is dry and warm and you must keep your health. If you don't, I will get in trouble, so drink one for yourself and one for me."

After we had unpacked and settled down somewhat, I told him that I had taught English to Chinese students for three years, and that his English was especially good. He gently bowed and thanked me, and in the manner of any good Chinese student, asked if I would teach him more. Not for the first time since leaving Malaysia more than a decade ago, I cursed myself for not having studied Mandarin so that I could get about here without having to rely on translation.

The Guest House, or *Diaoyutai*, is for VIPs, very clearly. It is where Nixon, Bush and Mondale all stayed during their visits here — and Alexander Haig will be a guest almost immediately after our departure (pity...). They all stayed in Villa #18, which allowed Mr. Wong to announce playfully, "so you are ahead of them."

There are two floors in each Villa. The rooms, which are not all the same, are immense, high-ceilinged, plush-carpeted suites. Two or three people have huge drawing rooms adjacent to their bedrooms. There are mahogany and jade treasures in these large sitting rooms, as well as the more spectacular art treasures that are in a very large meeting room off the hallway as you enter the Villa. Beautiful plants line the hallways.

In addition to this amazing desk on which I'm writing, with its collection of pens and ink, paper and envelopes, calendar and map (there is not a Gideon Bible in sight — or out of sight, for that matter), each room has a large cedar closet, two large wooden beds each covered with a maroon satin quilt, turned down invitingly, two sturdy wicker chairs, throw rugs and a television set. There is also a small refrigerator, which, as Mr. Wong said it would be, is filled to overflowing with a variety of drinks and fresh fruit.

At the same time, in the midst of all this opulence (which had us running up and down stairs checking out each other's accommodations to see who got the prize for the richest room, while exclaiming, over and over, "Is this the Peoples' Republic? Is this the place where the Revolution has brought down the mighty and brought up the meek? Is this China?"), there is a certain seedy quality that is very endearing.

Our bathroom, for example, has one of those attachable-detachable shower hoses — and no curtain. The tub is rust stained, and the toilet paper (Goldfish brand) is coarser than anything you'd find in America, even in a Greyhound station. It's more like paper towels than toilet paper. There is a chipped white porcelain cuspidor under the sink.

We were told by Mr. Wong that we are free to wander anywhere within the fenced compound, and that should any of us desire to go our own separate ways outside, there would be no problem as long as we obtained a pass from him beforehand so that "the soldiers at the door to the Guest House will let you in, or something like that." Mr. Wong throws in "or something like that" in the same way that some American teenagers punctuate their speech with "you know."

Tomorrow we are to have breakfast at 8:45, and then spend the day sightseeing (which, I'm sure, the UUSC wishes it had forbidden): Forbidden City, Tienanmen Square and the Summer Palace. Before breakfast, however, I hope to get up early enough to explore the compound to make sure that it meets with my approval.

I am in China! At the airport, after passing through the easiest customs and immigration check I've ever experienced (no one had to open a single bag), as we were walking out of the building into the night air of the People's Republic, I passed three customs officials sitting just inside, enjoying each other's company. They were deep in conversation, as they waited for the last of our motley crew to wander out, so that they could also go home to bed. Two sat side-by-side, while the third sat behind them, both his arms draped loosely and lovingly around the neck and shoulders of the young men sitting in front of him. It was a natural demonstration of friendship, an unselfconscious display of affection. We clumped by, self-consciously avoiding looking in their direction because of our own, prurient interpretations. Unknowingly transgressing our own cultural taboos, the young man in back stroked his friend's neck in unabashed tenderness, and I remembered, again, why I love being in the Orient.

May 29, Beijing: Diaoyutai

I awoke at six this morning, and went for a walk around the compound. Like the villa itself, it is a wonderful combination of extravagance and ruin. There are 18 villas on the grounds connected by paved roads and dirt walkways. Even at six a.m., the grounds are already bustling with the activity of construction, which is going on everywhere. There are beautiful, graceful trees in profusion (I wish I were able to identify them), and large ponds with gracefully arched stone bridges. In the middle of one is an octagonal pagoda with a double Chinese roof, like a tiered garden gazebo. The ponds are lily covered. Toward one entrance is a gigantic red billboard with Chinese writing whose characters I cannot read, but which are likely a quotation from Chairman Mao. Next to one arched bridge is a very tall flagpole from which the Red Flag can be seen from all parts of the compound.

Pagoda in lake, Diaoyutai

Around the perimeter of the grounds, a brick wall about 8-10 feet high prevents prying eyes from looking in, or looking out. By climbing up on various construction platforms and other low structures inside, I could see through the electrified wire that is strung along the top of the wall. I saw people, hundreds of people, Chinese all, moving in all directions, mostly by bicycle, but almost an equal number on foot. Most wear the ubiquitous Mao suit, all blue or all gray, though a very few sport more colorful shirts. Quite a large number, especially older people, can be seen slowly bending and unbending in the endless flow of Tai Chi exercises, like ballet dancers in slow motion.

There is a lake behind the compound, and, to my great surprise, there were at least two dozen boys and men (no women) in brief bathing suits swimming across it. There is a submerged platform from which they all begin their swim, and most go clear across and return. Others, less energetic this early in the morning, are playing in the canal that feeds the lake. Spanning the canal is a wonderful bridge, entirely constructed of bamboo. Below the bridge an old man is fishing with a large, tent-like net, shaped by its two long bamboo poles, lashed together and bowed. On the dirt path that completely surrounds the lake, a younger man is selling his morning's catch, anchovy-size fish spread on a cloth on the ground. Half a dozen bicyclists and walkers stand around haggling with him over price — a view of Chinese capitalism that is as familiar to me as a thousand similar scenes I encountered on the streets of Malaysia.

Fisherman casts his net (lower left) under bamboo bridge across canal behind *Diaoyutai*

Inside the compound, the wall is often buttressed with bamboo scaffolding, and there are numerous places in the wall that anyone could climb through. That no one does is probably due as much to habit as to the only armed soldier I ran across in the compound. He was standing next to one of the scaffoldings in an army-green Mao suit and cap with its large red star in the center. On the high collars of his jacket are stripes of red cloth sewn on. He looked very young, and held his rifle casually at his side. I came up to him and asked, in gestures, if I could take his picture. He put up his hand and shook his head vigorously, so I moved on.

But I didn't get the feeling that anything bad would happen if I did take his picture, either.

I discovered a smaller compound within the compound where the evidence of construction was strewn so haphazardly — an accident waiting to happen — that had this been an American construction site, the contractor would be inviting a lawsuit. This particular construction was to renovate several two-hundred-year-old living quarters so that they can be used for future foreign guests. The old buildings on the site are beautiful, with sloping tile roofs and red lacquered pillars.

There is a partly completed rock garden and pond in the middle of this self enclosed compound, and here I found a young man practicing his English by himself. His name is Mr. Sun, and he is guiding a group of American textile types around China. He invited me to go swimming with him tomorrow in the lake behind the *Diaoyutai*. Before I approached him and introduced myself, I listened to him repeating over and over again, in too-perfect English, "*Diaoyutai*, located on the western outskirts of Beijing, is on the site of an imperial hostel of the Qing Dynasty, and one of the best preserved centuries-old garden in the capital." As he read the same phrase again and again, I wondered if Mr. Wong was in some other part of the compound practicing as diligently. His English, though not as perfect in either pronunciation or syntax as that of Mr. Sun, sounds much more natural. In fact, its informal quality gives it the feeling of a native speaker. Perfect English by Americans, as Henry Higgins made clear, betrays the speaker as a non-native.

Besides inviting me to swim with him, Mr. Sun also invited me to stay and teach English here in Beijing. He seems certain that he could arrange for me to teach at his alma mater, the Foreign Language Institute. To my own great surprise, I heard myself declining the invitation. I'm not even sure why. There was a time when I would have given anything I had (spoken like a true pauper) to teach in China. Maybe this is just not the right time.

Perhaps because I accepted his offer to swim with him the next morning, Mr. Sun warmed to me. Examining the Chinese coin with its square hole that dangles from a necklace I have worn ever since it was given to me by an old man in Bali some years ago, he identified it as one from the Chien-Lung Dynasty, which makes it about as old as our Revolution.

On my way back to Villa #11, I went into the "shop" that is housed in one of the other villas. It had some beautiful crafts displayed, but all well beyond my means. I changed about $50 into Chinese yuan. There seem to be two kinds of money, because I received two different sized one-yuan notes, both in the identical reddish hue. The smaller of the two, no larger than Monopoly money, depicts a group of workers walking along carrying hoes, baskets, shovels and other tools.

There are an equal number of men and women. The other one (the other yuan) is closer to the size of our money, and has a woman driving a tractor on one side and man on horseback herding sheep on the other. The two-yuan note, which is green, depicts a huge bridge spanning a large river. I brought a total of $400 on this trip, which, I'm sure, would be considered insignificant by most of this group of well-heeled Americans. But it is more than I can really afford. My $50 bought me 86 yuan and change, which is measured in *Jiao* (ten to a yuan) and *Fen* (ten to a *Jiao*).

After my walk, during which I encountered not a single "foreigner," (or, as my Malaysian students referred to us, *fung mao kui* — red-headed devils), I returned to the villa in time for a sumptuous breakfast of eggs and delicious, but unidentifiable, meat. Dinni, our tour leader — the Harvard educated lawyer who doesn't practice — has said she will inquire as to the possibility of having a special table for those who are daring enough to want a Chinese breakfast (a number which does not exceed four people at the moment), and visions of dim sum dance in my head.

Just as when, fifteen years ago, I arrived in Tawau, the small town carved out of the jungle in Malaysian Borneo where I taught in a Chinese high school, I am under a magic spell here. All is beautiful. Unlike Tawau, however, I am not the only American around — and the group keeps impinging on my magic. For example, when I came into the dining hall this morning, I was the last to arrive, so had to take the only space available at a table where I might not have chosen to sit.

When I told my breakfast companions about Mr. Sun and his invitation to me to join him tomorrow at the lake for a swim, my breathless excitement was met with the clipped, staccato delivery of Mr. Polaroid, who said without equivocation or verb subjects, "No! Can't swim! Lake has parasites. Chinese immune. Glad you told me. Might have gone. Can't do it. Very important!" I can't tell which I resent more, the substance of his warning (would I have resented him less if he had said nothing and I had ended up with parasites?), or the I-know-more-than-you manner in which it was delivered. But prudence dictates, I suppose, that I will have to forego the possible parasite-producing pleasure of swimming with Mr. Sun. I wish I could feel grateful for the "knowledge," but I feel only resentment for his having interfered with my magic.

As Mr. Polaroid might put it, "Gotta go. Can't write more. Time to board the bus."

• •

It has been a dizzying, dazzling, frustrating and very tiring day, which isn't over yet.

The Forbidden City

After breakfast, we left for the Forbidden City in our air-conditioned tour bus. The wide streets are crowded with bicyclists, buses and even a few automobiles.

Across the street from the entrance to the Forbidden City, so-called because in ancient times, ordinary Chinese were forbidden to enter (like the State Guest House today) is Tienanmen Square, the gigantic plaza with its Great Hall of the People and Mao Tse Tung Memorial. Over the entrance to the City is a huge portrait of Chairman Mao, the first we have seen.

Walking into Forbidden City makes literal the cliché, "it takes your breath away." You walk into a huge courtyard surrounded by animal statuary (I fell in love with a ten ton bronze turtle). On the other side of the courtyard is a wide stone stairway leading into the first of what seems like an endless string of opulent temples with gilded roofs, separated from each other by large courtyards. Each temple is more splendid than the last. Under ornately tiled ceilings of blue and gold are the red or gold-pillared halls containing incredible art treasures.

The Forbidden City

In the Hall of Supreme Harmony lies a golden throne that looks like the sarcophagus of King Tut: a lattice-work of golden dragons over jade, about six feet long, covered with a plush golden cushion. In front of it lies a highly polished golden bejeweled stool. It is protected by a pair of jade elephants, one on each side, standing atop octagonal-shaped ebony tables. Intricate golden snakes seem to writhe along bas-relief panels that serve as the walls. In front of the Hall stands its protector: a huge bronze lion. There are magnificent tapestries on the walls, sedan chairs that Cleopatra would have envied, bronze cranes and dragons and lions, stone carvings, and, in the connecting courtyards, the paving stones themselves are carved with dragon and cloud designs. The upturned corners of the Chinese roofs are occupied by whole families of gargoyles. And the human crowds swarm everywhere.

Today, the King of Belgium (who is a neighbor of ours... he and his entourage are in Villa #18, of course) was also a visitor at the Forbidden City, swelling the size of the crowd. But Mr. Wong assured us that there are always crowds everywhere in Beijing, a city of nine million people. Of course, there are always large crowds of people in New York, too, but they aren't Chinese crowds. Where do all these Chinese come from?

Before we went through the deceptively simple, unadorned arched entrance to the City, Mr. Wong gathered us around him to tell us that the bus would drive to the back, where we would find it as we exited the Forbidden City at the other end. Because of the schedule, he said, we must be ready to board the bus by 11:45, so it is important that we all stick together. That last bit of advice — when it was inevitably ignored — would later turn Mr. Wong into a real person in my eyes, as opposed to a smiling tour guide. The real person it turned him into, as it happens, was a hot-tempered, angry man, and the object of his ire, among others, was none other than yours truly. Still, his display of righteous temper made him genuine — entirely scrutable — endeared him to me even as I withered under his outburst.

But I am getting ahead of myself.

The sheer immensity of the Forbidden City guaranteed that the group would not all proceed at the same pace, and we soon split into two contingents, advice to the contrary notwithstanding. I found myself in a small group of six people: Dinni, Kay, David Mintz (a staffer with the National Council on Crime and Delinquency from Hackensack), Pearl West (California's juvenile prison director), Aric and I. As we made our way from courtyard to courtyard and temple to temple (like the good Prince Prospero in Poe's "The Masque of the Red Death"), we assumed that the rest of the group was ahead of us. We emerged into a lovely, large garden filled with trees and rock sculptures.

The garden was also filled with people playing, talking, eating ice cream and laughing. We tarried for a while before going through the final temple, the Hall of Imperial Peace, and out the back where lines and lines of tour buses waited (and a fleet of shiny black limos to carry the King of Belgium and his entourage). Although we found our bus, we did not find our group. We were a little early, so we decided to keep walking to see if they had gone on ahead.

Before us lay a formidable hill with a pagoda-like temple at the summit. Presuming the others were there, we went on ahead and reached the top about twenty minutes later. It commanded a spectacular panorama of the Forbidden City below, with its gold-tiled rooftops, and of the city of Beijing itself, surprisingly flat and unspectacular. But the only people at the top — and there were many — were Chinese. One particularly obnoxious young man of about 20 followed close behind Kay all the way to the top, begging her in pantomime to take his picture with her Polaroid. Finally, Kay, who is perhaps the most compassionate and gentle soul on this trip, reacted — a measure of just how our miles-long morning excursion had exhausted us all. "I only take pictures of beautiful people," she snapped, surprising herself and me with her atypical vehemence. He smiled, uncomprehendingly, displaying rotting black teeth.

So, we climbed back down again, taking a different route from the one which had led us to the top. Still, we found no one at the bus.

Since we knew we had to be somewhere shortly after noon, and since it was still twenty minutes before twelve, we decided to wander back into the garden-park for one last lazy stroll, before returning to the bus to wait for the larger group to join us. Kay decided to stay on the bus.

We returned about fifteen minutes later. Kay was standing outside the bus looking very distressed. Everyone else was on the bus, except for Len Troppin, another NCCD staffer who is the assistant group leader, and Mr. Wong. They had gone back into Forbidden City in search of us, despite Kay's assurances that we would soon return. According to Kay, they had blood in their eyes when they left, and the group, she said, was ready to lynch us. More examples of just how tired we all are. And it's only day one!

When the six of us climbed onto the bus, our friends — lawyers, judges and jailers all — hissed at us. There was nothing friendly in it, either. Had this been a tour group of jocks instead of jurists, they would have wanted to fight. Dinni, as group leader, got the worst of it. Her explanation and apology were drowned out in a chorus of hissing and angry outbursts.

When Messers Wong and Troppin returned, which was almost immediately, the bus departed. Neither said a word. Mr. Wong, whose running commentaries we had already come to expect, sat in brooding silence for most of the way. At last, he rose and told us that he had arranged for us to take a boat across a lake to the Summer Palace, and that our late return had put that excursion in peril. He had told us to stay together, he reminded, and we had failed to do that. So, he added angrily, the six people who had wandered off by themselves, and especially the leader herself, would bear the responsibility for aborting the Summer Palace outing if, indeed, it had to be aborted.

From the reaction of the group, one would have thought that they had all come to China for the express purpose of checking out the Summer Palace (which, I venture to say, only one or two of us had ever heard of the day before).

Of course, we had not returned late, but rather had left again after returning early. That explanation went unheard, however, or at least did nothing to lessen the palpable tension on the bus.

What accomplished that was the cooling bus ride to the lake. As it turned out, we got there in time for our appointed boat ride across a lake absolutely jammed with row boats near the shore, lying low in the water because each was filled with laughing people. They happily bumped into each other, using their oars to push away. Farther out into the lake, the row boats were able to free themselves from the congested shores, and we passed boats with as many as ten people in them, as well as many with couples, rowing leisurely, usually sitting under parasols.

Our boat was a large, flat-bottomed thing. It had benches along either side, and was covered with a flat, wooden roof. In the back, the flat roof gave way to a Chinese roof covering a square gazebo, and behind this extended a wooden platform. On this platform stood an old man in baggy gray pants, a comfortable looking long-sleeved white cotton shirt, black Chinese cloth shoes and a straw hat. He smiled a toothless smile, and pushed off from the shore with a long bamboo pole.

The photographers went wild! Half a dozen Polaroids were whipped out, as one by one, they stood next to him and asked another in the group to take two photos. As the image of each initial photo emerged, the picture taker handed it to the old man, a memento of this momentous moment in his life. He barely glanced at the pictures as he put them in his shirt pocket, one after another, undoubtedly to join hundreds of others at home. Occasionally, he pushed with one foot on a wooden stick at his feet, which was connected to the rudder, and we turned.

Boat congestion on lake at the Summer Palace

Once free of the bumper-to-bumper rowboat traffic that clumped together around the embarkation ramp, we were pulled by a power boat, of sorts. It chugged and sputtered and spat along the edge of the lake, which was dotted by huge pagodas and temples, aflame with golden yellow tiles.

After about ten minutes, we disembarked alongside a gigantic, gravity-defying marble boat, which had been built by some former emperor or empress, whose name escapes me. It actually floats. We had lunch in a wonderful old restaurant where, it is said, the emperors came to listen to the singing of the orioles.

We heard no orioles, though, and we saw no emperors. In fact, except for those serving our meals and the occasional guide, we saw no Chinese people at all.

I banished this disturbing realization, however, in order to better enjoy the incredible spread that was laid before us. There were steaming dishes of chicken and fish, endless vegetable dishes that none of us recognized, boiled rice and fried rice, pork dishes that I took more than my share of, and copious quantities of Shin Tao beer. Add to this the fruit snack Mr. Wong had given us on the bus to the Forbidden City (a sticky, chewy, fruity candy, like jujubes), which we ate all morning long, and you begin to appreciate how well fed we are and how fat we are becoming.

After lunch, we wandered outside, where the irrepressible Karamoko, our excon life of the party, donned an ancient Chinese emperor's costume — for a price and posed for the gawking tourists. I got a lovely picture of him in his orange silk robe surrounded by a gaggle of laughing Americans snapping picture after picture — the same group of Americans who had, oh so recently, been hissing and booing us, their traveling companions.

Ex-prisoner Karamoko Baye in rented emperor's robe at Summer
Palace (Tour leader Dinni Gordon, top right)

We walked back to the bus over beautiful bridges along the water's edge, amidst crowds of Chinese tourists, and I wondered where they had eaten their lunches. We saw where the Dowager Wu Xi had squandered the royal treasure on her Epicurean debauches (a dowager after my own heart), where she stuffed herself on Chinese delicacies, dressed herself in Chinese silk robes, where she slept, held court and watched the opera. (She had a special hall built for her use only to watch her beloved Chinese opera, one of the few forms of music for which I have never developed an ear to appreciate).

By this time, of course, we were getting a little punchy. It was 1:30, and we had consumed a huge amount of food, and drunk enough beer to float the marble boat. No matter. We reboarded the bus and headed for Peking University, where we were to spend three hours discussing China's new criminal code with its creators and interpreters, the faculty of the Law School. Our first official visit.

•••

The Great Helmsman, Chairman Mao oversees Beijing University

The Law School, Beijing University

We arrived at the appointed hour, and were met by members of the faculty. In front of the library building, is a towering statue of Chairman Mao. The Chairman, imposing in his huge stone coat, stares out across the campus with his hands behind his back, like Winston Churchill. Later —after our session with the law school lawyers — we all crowded around the base of the statue to have our pictures taken. We were told not to miss this opportunity, because the statue would probably soon be coming down. No explanation was provided.

Before this, however, we met for two hours in a very modest room, sitting at a long table, we on one side and the law faculty on the other, facing each other and sipping tea from gorgeous tall white and blue porcelain mugs with lids.

First, we listened to the formal presentation of the law faculty, with Mr. Wong translating, rather feebly I felt, though, of course, I could not understand the Chinese. We heard how the new code has brought together a collection of disparate laws, and, for the first time, articulated a clear set of legal principles. The professors told us that in the wake of the Cultural Revolution that had wreaked such havoc on the system (and which had forced them into exile in the countryside), the law schools were attempting the monumental task of educating enough lawyers and judges to carry out the mandates of the new code, which are: to support the dictatorship of the proletariat, to defend the socialist system, and to help maintain public ownership of property, as opposed to the capitalist legal system with its heavy emphasis on the defense of private property.

After this, we were invited to ask questions. It was here that the fatigue we were all feeling moved me to frustration and anger, though repressed and contained. What became immediately clear was that there were not only two distinct views of the American criminal justice system present on our side of the table (and many gradations of those views), but that only one was going to get a full airing. That view is best represented by Pearl West, head of California's state juvenile prison system, and Federal Judge Francis Bader-Mann (not his real name) whom Kay, Aric and I had already begun referring to as Judge B.M. You've heard this view before. It is that America, after all, is the hope of the world, the land of the free, the last bastion of equal justice under law, etc. It is a view of American superiority well illustrated by an incident that happened earlier in the day.

After stuffing ourselves at the oriole restaurant, we had emerged into a small courtyard (where Karamoko had posed, berobed), crowded with the other white tourists we had seen in the restaurant. A middle-aged American woman from another tour group caught a glimpse of my NMPC tote bag with its legend, "Jobs Not Jails," looked at me in an accusatory way, and snapped, "Does that mean you don't want anyone in jail?"

Stuffed and lethargic, and not wanting to get into a major discussion, I replied, "Well, not exactly, but close enough."

"Well," she sniffed, "I certainly don't think you should be spreading that idea about in China!" To which I, and the three tall glasses of beer I had imbibed at lunch, replied, "Frankly, I don't care much what you think."

This, of course, was too much for the irate, law-abiding lady who announced to all within earshot, "I'll definitely never take another People-to-People trip."

"That's a good idea," I said, getting the last word.

Unfortunately, at the law school, the point of view she represented seemed to prevail on our side of the table, despite the overwhelming number of liberal types among us, including the person leading the tour. Judge B.M. offered to "help the Chinese," and went into some detail explaining the salient score factors characteristic of the federal sentencing guidelines recently reproduced by a number of states. (Under those guidelines, watch out if you are black, brown, unemployed, or have, by some strange coincidence, ever had a brush with the law.) He spoke again and again about our being "a model system."

Pearl talked about our "model" juvenile justice system. She's eminently qualified to do so, presiding as she does, over the nation's largest prison system for kids — overwhelmingly black and brown. She said that the underlying rationale of our juvenile justice system, *in loco parentis*, was failing, and therefore we were necessarily locking up more kids. But, and she emphasized this point, the number we lock up still represents a tiny fraction of the total number we process through the criminal justice system. She said nothing about the substandard schooling or the rampant violence that infects these California kiddie prisons where nearly 10,000 children are held in cages designed for half that number.

There was no mention of our social decay, our lack of opportunity for large segments of the population, our total failure to "promote the general welfare," in the broadest sense of those words in our Constitution's Preamble, until much, much later. Dinni finally mentioned the problem of unemployment and its connection to our justice system after repeated prodding (I kept passing her notes). The word "racism" never passed anyone's lips. Indeed, one could have gotten the impression by listening to the assembled, that we have a working system to be emulated, a system that serves the ends of justice, rather than the ends of politicians. No one mentioned the fact that our "model system" already imprisons a greater percentage of its population than any country on earth, except for the Soviet Union and South Africa. No one talked about the significance of our caging more and more poor and minority people in any direct way. No one talked about the recidivism rate in "progressive" California — three out of four will return to prison after release — or the fact that the Youth Authority, over which Pearl presides, acts like a direct funnel into the adult prison system. I didn't; Kay didn't; Karamoko didn't — though we all knew better.

After dinner tonight, there is to be a discussion of this problem. We've got to find some way to allow the diversity represented in this group to be expressed, openly and officially, or I'll scream, openly and unofficially. There also has to be some mechanism for dealing with some of the highly technical questions that are of keen interest to one or two (the statisticians among us), but not to most.

I should point out, by way of digression, that my view of Judge Bader-Mann was already pretty well formed by breakfast, as I'm sure was his of me. As I emerged from my room this morning, I watched him and Mrs. B.M. giving instructions to two young women employees of the Guest House about their laundry. It was clear, to me at least, that both women had a fine grasp of English. That fact, however salient though it was, did not deter the good judge from starring in the role of Ugly American.

"We've left our laundry in room 202," he said. "It must be washed in cold water. Do you understand?" They nodded. "Cold, not hot," he continued. "Brrrr," he said, embracing himself and rubbing his own arms in mock cold. "Do you understand?"

Clearly, they did. "Yes," both said, again and again.

"Cold, not hot," he repeated, going through the charade yet again.

This went on for at least five minutes, until the judge was thoroughly satisfied that his simple message was understood by the foreigners. He turned in my direction to walk to breakfast. Mrs. B.M. walked close beside him, and — through tight lips that barely moved — she stage whispered, "I told you to smile when you talk to them!"

Then, on the bus to Forbidden City this morning, I got a reminder of my place. I was turned around in my seat, talking to Aric behind me while Mr. Wong was making an announcement. Suddenly, I felt an unceremonious poke in the back from the dignified Judge B.M., along with the pointed suggestion that I shut up. "Shut up, David," he said. I did.

....

We dealt with all the previously-discussed problems in a muted way in an after-dinner meeting at which it was decided that questions would be submitted in advance to pre-selected questioners, designated by Dinni before each meeting.

A rumor is spreading, especially by former Peace Corps lawyer, Bill Josephson, that People-to-People may have failed to coordinate effectively with the Chinese Ministry of Justice. He and others are expressing concern that the Ministry may only be minimally involved in this tour, which could result in aspects of the system we hope to examine, People's Courts for example, being severely limited. I am frankly skeptical of this point of view, though I confess I base my opinion more on the fact that we are staying here at the *Diaoyutai*, the government Guest House, than anything else. Tomorrow may tell, though. After visiting Beijing Municipal Prison in the morning, we have a scheduled afternoon meeting with representatives of the Ministry of Justice. We shall see.

But getting back to the here and now — and something of great importance to me — tonight's all vegetarian dinner outdid itself. Not only was each course more delicious than the one before — asparagus and walnuts, spring rolls, water chestnuts, a savory fungus called monkey hair, Chinese peas and mushrooms, and much, much more — but it was also punctuated by numerous toasts with the powerful rice wine, *maotai*. The toasting was inaugurated by our host for the evening, another Mr. Wong who is responsible for all the construction inside the compound. (Can you imagine his hard-hat counterpart in America ever being asked to host such an affair?)

Between toasts, he gave each of us a brocade pillow case depicting the Guest House in greens, reds and yellows. We toasted Dinni, the entire group, our own Mr. Wong, etc.

Halfway through the festivities, I was again overwhelmed by the realization — the re-realization — that we're eating this most incredible food, getting drunk on this most incredible wine, and feeling this most incredible ache in our ankles and feet from walking in the People's Republic of China! More than the rice wine, that knowledge goes to my head.

And now I must repair to my suite, put my tired and slightly inebriated body between cool sheets and under satin spreads to sleep, perchance to dream.

May 30, Beijing Municipal Prison

The day has been one of contrasts, which I cannot spend time to describe now. In just twenty minutes we leave, again, for a Hunanese feast and a Tibetan opera.

Suffice it to say that the faces of the men and women in Beijing Municipal Prison will haunt me for many days to come. Chinese men with close-cropped hair returning silent stares. White-capped women bent over their sewing. The deafening silence.

I am counting on the upcoming meal (which, I hope, is not upcoming after it is down going) and entertainment to bring my spirits back up. I feel like a yo-yo about to be yoed.

· ·

The opera was wonderful, if you like that sort of thing. I love the splendor of it more than the music itself. It reminded me of many I have seen in Japan, filled with colorful dancers swinging amply costumed behinds from side to side in stylized postures, while good triumphs over evil. It was fun.

Before the opera, we had yet another in an unending line of feasts. This one was a Hunanese special, which, like Szechuan cooking, is deliciously spicy. Like the others, it was superb. The one strange thing about it, and about the opera and the lunch yesterday (and, I bet, the Peking duck tomorrow) is that there were only western tourists in the restaurants and mostly tourists in the theater. It's hard to tell whether this catering to tourists has pushed Chinese out of places, or whether the places themselves have been created for tourists. In either case, I find myself more and more uncomfortable with the arrangement.

Today was a very strange day. We've done and seen so much that it's hard to believe we've been here only two days. Perhaps it will become less overwhelming after a while, but for now, it's hard to take it all in and sort it all out. Let me try.

The prison tour was truly mind-bending. We were taken en masse through the prison, which is located right in the heart of a residential area, so unlike American prisons which are mostly out-of-sight-out-of-mind. From the outside, it's hard to tell it's a prison at all. There is an imposing rock wall with an arched doorway, over which is a giant red star, and two police kiosks on either side of it. But, with its flower carvings and graceful columns, it looks more like the entrance to a municipal garden than a municipal prison. Once inside the doorway, however, you know it's a prison.

Residential neighborhood next to Beijing Municipal Prison

It was built by the British shortly after the turn of the 19th Century, and it looks it. Its long, low buildings are made of gray bricks, with gray tile roofs and corrugated tin awnings. The grounds are very clean. We saw virtually no prisoners anywhere outside the buildings, but the guards were everywhere.

This prison houses 1900 prisoners, including 350 women. But it's hard to imagine where all 1900 might be. We saw, perhaps, 600 men and women in various stages of making socks: spinning and weaving the cotton yarn, putting it over metal forms, sorting, etc. There are, the warden told us at the briefing afterwards, more than sixty separate processes in the manufacture of socks. We saw women prisoners at work, row after row of them, in large, dark warehouse-like rooms, sewing men's trousers on electric machines. Just above their heads were double fluorescent lights, and above them a long banner probably extolling the virtue of serving the people through labor. They wore white uniforms and white caps, and the only sound you could hear was the hum of the light fixtures and the whir of the sewing machines. None of the prisoners uttered a sound.

We saw the cells, where ten prisoners sleep, five side-by-side on each of two plywood boards on the floor separated by a narrow aisle that runs from front to back. These wooden planks in the men's cells were covered with Japanese tatami matting, while those in the women's cells were covered with a slightly softer cotton material. The cells were spotless. Five sets of bedding were neatly folded and placed side-by-side on each plank, below towels hanging on a wire stretched across the cell. A broom stood in one corner. In the wall opposite the heavy steel door was a small barred window.

We saw the infirmary where prisoners were being treated, many with acupuncture. We saw the spotless, but ancient kitchen, with its huge wooden vats and wooden cooking utensils that look like they belong to a family of giants. Two black-clad male prisoners, also wearing white caps, stirred a steaming cauldron.

And we saw prisoners making pink plastic children's shoes. Some looked up from their work just long enough to return our stares.

Our cameras clicked away incessantly, like tourists at the Great Wall (where we go tomorrow). For me, it was a mixture of excruciating pain, knowing that public humiliation is one of the greatest hurts a Chinese can suffer, and excruciating and sordid curiosity, a wish to see more as I wished to be away.

I wanted to stop those who invaded the infirmary with their cameras flashing everywhere, without a thought for the privacy of the man lying face down on the table, with needles protruding from his bare butt.

I could not move as quickly as the group, and was continually hurried along by the guards, both men and women. In their blue trousers and white shirts with red stripes on the collars, they reminded me of officious busboys in Chinatown.

Having experienced so many American prison tours where visitors avoid eye contact, as if among lepers, I made a point of smiling at the prisoners, and a few of the young ones — smiled back. But most were older, and they looked tough, unsmiling, defiant. The guards smiled — especially the old ones — but it was the smile I've seen so many times before — the guarded smiles of prison guards. One of the women guards, one who refused to leave my side as I trailed farther and farther behind the main group, reminded me of the woman villain in "From Russia, With Love". There was a quiet, even sadistic menace in her look.

There were long, dark hallways down which we were forbidden to travel. We saw no isolation cells; we heard no prisoners speak.

When we reassembled in the meeting room outside the warden's office, young women in white served us tea, then stood at the back of the room. The warden took his place at the front of the room to answer our questions. By now, I wanted to cry out, to run away. I felt the same choking feeling I have when I visit a prison at home. And while I struggled to keep these emotions in check, the group began by applauding the warden for his cooperation.

We had designated Carl Berry, the associate warden of Greenhaven Prison in New York, as the official questioner for this visit. Carl knows prisoners, and he asked good questions, many of which had been submitted to him by others in the group.

We learned that there is only this prison and one youth reformatory serving this city of nine million people, far fewer than a city of comparable size in America would serve, though other prisoners may be housed in other, more distant places. We learned that the largest proportion of the prison population was there for non-violent property offenses, which surprised most of us. That, of course, is also true for American prisons. We learned that the average age of Chinese prisoners is 35, which is considerably higher than the average age of American prisoners (23), and that the average time served is also much longer — about five years versus about two in the federal system in the United States. We learned that prisoners are allowed one visit a month and one, or, at most, two letters.

But we were also told many things by the warden that I found difficult, if not impossible, to believe. For example, when we asked if prisoners were forced to observe a rule of silence (which was true in American prisons of the last century, and in some American prisons right up until recent times), he replied that there was no such rule. "The prisoners were just showing their respect," he said, between drags on his cigarette. "We educate them before your arrival to be respectful."

Maybe. But coupled with some other highly dubious assertions he made — reinforced by my experience with the duplicity of American corrections officials — I doubt the validity of what we were told, extrapolating from what we saw.

I'll tell you about some of those dubious assertions tomorrow. I'm fading fast now.

May 31, Beijing: Post-prison Q&A

It is cooler today as I sit on the low rock wall in front of Villa #11 and try, quickly, to complete my description of yesterday's prison visit. I fell asleep while trying to write last night, and have only an hour and a half before breakfast. After breakfast, The Great Wall of China, where we will picnic, visit the Ming Tombs, and, perhaps, have a free hour in the afternoon to shop and walk around.

I was describing the hour or so talk we had with Warden Xin after our tourof the Beijing Municipal Prison. Some of his answers to Greenhaven Warden Carl Berry's questions left me feeling as if I were being lied to, the same way I feel after trying to get information from the Federal Bureau of Prisons in our own capital.

For example, in answer to a specific question about the problem of sexual assault, Warden Xin said, "There is no homosexuality in this prison. We encourage the right thinking. Homosexuality is immoral, and it does not go on here." Considering the sleeping arrangements — what Aric described as "a daisy-chain waiting to happen" — my own three-year experience among the Chinese in Malaysia, and what I know of what it means to be human, I simply do not believe this. Hearing the giggles and seeing the furtive looks exchanged by the staff during the warden's answer, and especially the female tea servers in the back of the room, only confirms my doubts.

Another claim that I find hard to accept at face value is that gambling is not a problem in this prison. If I knew nothing about the Chinese, I could conceivably believe this claim. But I do know something about the Chinese, and what I know leads me to conclude that this is as fantastic a claim as the one denying the existence of homosexuality. Even acknowledging the gross generalization of this observation, most of the Chinese I know are inveterate gamblers, beginning in childhood. In the cloistered atmosphere of a prison, I would expect gambling to flourish — unless, of course, it is forcefully repressed.

Finally, his self-serving answer to the question about prison violence — there is none, ever, against authorities, and only very rarely against other prisoners — left me thinking that a warden is a warden is a warden (with apologies to Carl Berry), and a prison is a prison is a prison.

Incidentally, the prison visit is not the only thing that happened yesterday. We also met with the Ministry of Justice, both the entire group as well as a smaller, five-person delegation, of which I was one.

But, it is time for breakfast. So, with my priorities firmly established, I will tackle first things first.

•••••••••••••••••••••••••••••••••••••

Ministry of Justice

With another huge breakfast (crab, apple fritters, peanuts, boiled eggs) under my literally expanding belt, I have just a few minutes to finish my description of yesterday's activities before embarking on today's.

After the prison tour, we came back to the Guest House for lunch, after which we met with five members of the Ministry of Justice. The meeting was here at the *Diaoyutai* in a huge room that might have served as a small ballroom, especially as it was arranged with dozens of overstuffed chairs and sofas pushed up against the walls. Every few feet there is a round or square table, each with an ashtray. Chinese paintings and scrolls adorn the walls. The very high ceiling gives the room a cavernous effect.

It was decided before they came that a five-person delegation would meet with them after the group meeting to see if we could put to rest the rumors that the Ministry is unwilling to help us to see a People's Court in action, a mediation process, and a local police department — things which we were led to believe had already been arranged by People-to-People. Some even have hopes of getting into a prison labor farm, though that has never been promised by anyone. The five of us representing the group will include both group leaders, Dinni and Len Troppin, former Federal Judge Arthur Lane (who was also formerly the Chair of NCCD), Bill Josephson (who gives an air of knowing everything, or believing he does), and me, because I am the only person in the group with experience living among the Chinese (though I don't see what special qualification this confers on me in this situation).

I found the large group meeting with the Ministry somewhat disturbing because most of the time was spent asking questions about things which we should have learned by reading the literature we received before the trip: who appoints judges, how does the appellate process work, and so forth. Despite being told that prisons do not fall within the Justice Ministry's jurisdiction but that of the Ministry of

Public Security, we spent a lot of time asking about prison policy, only to be told again and again to address those questions to the appropriate Ministry.

It was not until near the end of the meeting that anyone asked what the goals of the Ministry of Justice are. "We are resolved, determined to establish the rule of law, provide the lawyers and judges to implement the rule of law, and to strengthen the socialist revolution," answered Mr. Yi of the Foreign Affairs Bureau. Perhaps reflecting on his own exile during the turbulent Cultural Revolution, he added passionately and, at least to us, surprisingly, "We simply cannot afford the disruption of the last ten years. We must rebuild after the destruction of the Gang of Four. We must construct the society."

Having seen to what lengths the law can be used to oppress — even in "the land of the free" — I do not share the same enthusiasm that "establishing the rule of law" will make for a just society. (I do not believe that Due Process of Law, for example, sanctifies the death penalty, whether in the United States or here.) On the other hand, these Chinese jurists are guided by recent personal experience with lawlessness, something which I have not experienced and do not envy.

At any rate, I found the smaller meeting more productive. Mr. Yi had a wonderfully infectious laugh. When I complimented him on his excellent English, he clearly reveled in my flattery while denying having any facility at all (Asian modesty), adding that he might have said the same for my Chinese. (I have been practicing the Mandarin phrase, "*Wo bu hui saw Chunguo wha*" — which I'm sure is the wrong way to say "I don't speak Chinese.")

After sparring for a while about the difficulties of setting up anything on such short notice, Yi promised to phone ahead to his colleagues in other cities on our itinerary to see if they could facilitate our requests. He stressed that he was unable to do anything about our wish to see a prison farm or a police department, which are outside his bailiwick, but that he would do all he could to let us see a People's

Court in action and to meet with a local lawyers' committee. It was clear that he had no intention of interceding on our behalf with the Ministry of Public Security. Regarding our Ministry of Justice interests, he said, "I will try to help you, but I can promise you nothing because these things take months to arrange."

Dinni suggested that the Ministry of Justice was not taking us seriously enough, which obviously annoyed Mr. Yi. I shared his annoyance. Her protest suggests an overblown sense of our own importance — and left me with a lingering suspicion that Dinni herself, as group leader, failed to lay the proper groundwork for this tour. All of this is speculative though, and we may yet get to see what we are hoping to see.

Mr. Yi and the four other Ministers agreed to meet us tonight for Peking duck, an occasion that Dinni and Bill Josephson have said they are going to use to press our case for introductions to the Ministry of Public Security. (I will be pressing my duck.) I think they're wasting their time, but it is Bill's idea, and I have yet to hear Dinni disagree with anything he has suggested regarding the tour. On the other hand (or, perhaps, it's the same hand), they have a playfully quarrelsome relationship about personal things, which reveals a longstanding friendship.

In fact, I've decided that Dinni's eagerness to defer to others reflects her unwillingness or inability actually to lead. I know many people with great, even inspiring, ideas who seem incapable of putting them into practice. Being a great thinker is different from implementing great thoughts. I think that is the reason, for example, that the "true blue" view of America was virtually the only one expressed at the law school yesterday. It is obvious that Dinni's political and social thinking are very close to mine. But she seems unable to take the lead — a failing that is glaringly clear in her present role.

···

Ming Tombs and Great Wall of China

I'm beginning to feel that the professional visits and tourist attractions on our agenda are only secondary to what really counts in this country — eating! The day began with another abundant breakfast, which, at least for me, included such delicious Chinese delicacies as 1,000-year-old egg and *lop cheong* — Chinese sausage. One breakfast table has been designated "the Chinese table," and there are always four or five adventurers to be found there. So far, Dinni and I are the only two regulars. The day ended — officially — with Peking duck. We have eaten enough for five emperors for a week.

Sandwiched between these culinary high points were other noteworthy diversions, like the Ming Tombs and The Great Wall of China.

After breakfast, we drove to the Ming Tombs, north of the city. There are thirteen such tombs in China, not all in the same area. The one we visited was built more than 500 years ago. Though the countryside is virtually flat right up to the site of the tombs, themselves, the backdrop is of impressively rugged mountains. The Ming emperors chose sites like this one, about 40 kilometers from Beijing, because they commanded an imposing view in front, and were protected by the mountains in back. The last of the Ming Tombs was built 150 years before our Revolution.

The hot, dry air and the mountainous topography had the eerie effect of conjuring up entire memories of events from my childhood that I didn't even know were there. Have you ever been walking down the street when you smell something that suddenly triggers a whole flood of memories? That was the feeling I had as I walked around the Tombs, and later, too, as the bus climbed into the mountains behind them. It felt like the small valley town in Southern California where I grew up; it felt like Ojai.

The Tomb itself was impressive, with its huge stone walls, its magnificent white porcelain urns with their encircling blue dragons, its intricately-carved stone slab thrones, its hidden entrances, its antiquity. But, to be honest, I'm not much moved by the tombs of kings. What moved me, besides the general feel of the land, were the grounds between the bus parking lot and the entrance to the Tombs. It was not the beauty of the place that moved me — bare earth and unspectacular trees interspersed with square stone tables and benches — but the Chinese activity taking place inside it.

Mr. Wong gave us only fifteen minutes to wander around after seeing the Tombs, but for me it was the most rewarding fifteen minutes of this excursion. While hordes of mostly white tourists happily made their way back to their waiting buses, I found a group of Chinese teenagers sitting at one of the stone tables playing cards. I looked. They looked. Almost immediately they summoned me to sit on the bench next to the dealer, who moved over slightly to accommodate me. I didn't require a second invitation. I sat and watched while they insistently offered me pieces of cake and cookies from the bag they had, and continued their game. To my real surprise, it is a game I know. It is the same game my own Malaysian Chinese students played; I have played it with Chin Ah Moi and Lim Nyun Chung and Liaw Fung Kong.

High schoolers invite me to join them at this familiar card game at
Ming Tombs

"*Dap yee,*" said one of the kids, triumphantly slamming down a deuce
on top of another, and picking up the pair. Again I was flooded with
memories of another time and place. "*Dap sam,*" the girl sitting next to
him said, throwing down a three of spades. I would have played with
them if there had been more time — it's a simple game of collecting
pairs — but Lynn Zeller signaled for me to get my ass in gear. Lynn,
who used to work for the NCCD in Hackensack is now with the
Kansas Corrections Department. While my new young friends
protested that I should stay and play, I stood, took their picture, and
departed with a wave.

I had spoken no Chinese to them and they had spoken no English
to me, but we had laughed together with familiar ease. I felt at home,
warmed before boarding the air-conditioned bus again for the ascent

to The Great Wall. Before getting back on the bus, where Mr. Wong would pass out ice-cream bars to cool us, I had to pee. (My morning coffee is the one link to an American breakfast I won't give up.)

I looked around and saw an open-air urinal off to one side, behind the stone building that houses an exhibit of the excavation of the Tomb and artifacts taken from it. I walked over to the cement rectangular slab on the ground with another slab, no higher than a small boy, rising left to right across its length. Another cement slab lay on the other side of this low wall. Each slab on the ground tilted toward the wall in the middle where a trough collected the urine, which flowed into holes in the trough. About half a dozen men stood on either side of the median. Although I felt rather conspicuous being not only the tallest man in either row, but also the only non-Asian person peeing there among all those Chinese men, none of them, either those next to me or those facing me from the other side, paid me any attention at all.

Behind the men facing me was a natural rock wall with occasional writing, apparently Chinese graffiti. Although Mr. Wong was standing next to the man next to me, I waited until we had both left the urinal to ask what the Chinese characters meant, a question which obviously flustered him. "Just some bad things," he said in a way that told me I should ask no more about it.

On our way from the Tomb, the bus stopped for a "photo opportunity" with the huge stone animals that line both sides of the road leading in. There were elephants and camels, horses and lions. I had my picture taken with four adorable little urchins next to a frightening looking gargoyle. A wooden wagon from the olden days, drawn by two horses, clip-clopped down the road toward where, I could not tell, but I got the distinct impression that it was not part of the tourist exhibits.

Four gorgeous children pose with two gargoyles (one in red T-shirt)
guarding road to Ming Tombs

Then we began the long climb into the mountains. The road was winding and passed small villages and streams and irrigation ditches. Up and up we went, until, still far from the top, we caught our first glimpse of that incredible wall. Like driving around a corner in South Dakota to catch your first sight of Mount Rushmore, it's hard to take your eyes off it. As more and more of its immensity comes into view, you become less and less able to adjust to what you are seeing. It's the kind of world wonder that the phrase "mind-blowing" was invented to describe. What words can adequately convey a 3500-mile wall, visible from space, built 2200 years ago but still structurally sound, stretching from horizon to horizon along high, rugged mountains? There are none.

Horse-drawn wagon on road to Ming Tombs

When I looked at The Great Wall, I remembered hearing an American tourist at the Grand Canyon say to her husband, "Well, it's certainly pretty." And I thought, "What a pale word 'pretty' is to describe this." Then I tried thinking of an adjective that wasn't pale. When Tricky Dick Nixon saw The Wall, he is said to have said, "Well, it certainly is great!" I guess, like the comment of that woman at the Grand Canyon, that is the definitive statement on the subject.

Before climbing The Wall, we ate a picnic lunch (naturally). In this case, "picnic lunch" translated as a box lunch, which we ate in another of those places where you see only other Americans, or, at least, no Chinese. There was a kind of carnival quality to the immediate surroundings, in the seediest sense of the word. The tables we ate at were crowded tightly together so that as many tourists as possible could squeeze in for their picnic lunches. All around us were shelves displaying souvenirs of all kinds: pennants, knickknacks, postcards and film. Outside was a large parking area that looked like the site of a bus convention, though the unpaved lot was a little muddy from an earlier rain. A steady stream of buses was entering through a short tunnel, which we had to walk back through in the opposite direction to get to the steps leading to the top of The Wall. At those steps there was a much smaller parking lot and several more concession stands. There were also a couple of buses in this lot, but it was apparently reserved for real VIPs because there was also a fleet of limousines. Again, the King of Belgium was crossing our path.

The sense of the tourist hustle is immediately, though not completely, dispelled when you climb The Wall — despite the fact that you are, of course, surrounded by other tourists (including many Chinese). The steps leading up to The Wall to the right are supposed to be "the easy way" and the ones to the left "the hard way." Both ways climb towards steep peaks, though, so it's hard to tell just what makes one way hard or easy. Chinese mythology has it, Mr. Wong explained, that if you take the easy way, you cannot be "a true man." So, the women led the way — the hard way, that is. Or, at least most of them did.

We climbed. Then we climbed some more. We climbed for about an hour.

Sometimes it was so steep, you could only go a few feet before having to stop and rest. Sometimes it was gently sloping. The final ascent onto The Wall itself is made by way of a short stairway. The countryside immediately on both sides of The Wall is both rugged and lush with vegetation, though way off it seemed dry and barren. The mountains look impassible enough to have kept out any potential invaders, and I wondered about the real utility of The Wall, a project that took one fifth of the working population to construct, according to the literature.

There are occasional reminders of the tourist a hustle even on The Wall. For the first time since arriving, I saw kids hawking their wares:

purported to be old coins and precious stones. The kids looked surprisingly like the urchins I had seen in Mexico. There was also a camel on a dirt road just below one of the castle-like turrets that punctuate the length of The Wall as far as you can see in either direction, some with stairways like the one that had taken us to the top. For a buck or so, you could have your picture taken astride the dromedary. Who would climb The Great Wall of China in order to have his picture taken on a camel, you ask. Our very own Karamoko, that's who!

Associate Prison Warden Carl Berry on The Great Wall of China

Finally, we retraced our steps, climbed back down, and, with some difficulty, found our bus. (All those East German buses look alike.) Those who had gone "the easy way" insisted that it had been the hard way. Those who had gone "the hard way" — especially the women — kept repeating, "I'm a true man!"

In fact, one of the "I-am-a-true-man" women and I had a rather ugly little exchange of words shortly thereafter.

I should preface this by admitting that I already harbored less than positive thoughts about Ellen before we had our tiff. She is a young, pretty lawyer married to a young, handsome lawyer. She works for the City of New York as one of the keepers of women in its sprawling jail system. He works for a foundation, evaluating various criminal justice programs funded by it. He is Steven Kelban who describes himself as a "liberal" who believes that by traveling the same circles the "decision-makers" travel, he can ultimately influence their decisions in a positive way. She is Ellen Shall, and describes herself as a "liberal" who apparently believes, because of that fact, that her role as the chief assistant to the head jailer of New York City women is beyond reproach. They were both public defenders once upon a time, but have now moved into far more lucrative positions. Each has spent more money already than I brought for the entire trip. But never mind.

Mr. Wong was explaining the rest of the day's agenda when Ellen interrupted to yell, from near the back of the bus, that she wanted to be dropped downtown, and that she wanted Mr. Wong to write the Guest House address so that she could take a taxi back. Mr. Wong explained that we were already very tired, which we were, and that we had an evening of activity planned. He suggested that it would be wiser to return and get some rest before dinner. "If you won't drop me downtown," Ellen said, "then I want you to arrange a taxi to pick me up at the Guest House so I can go into town and shop." This back and forth went on for some time before Mr. Wong gave up, defeated.

Perhaps remembering how vociferous she had been in denouncing the splinter group at Forbidden City, I leaned across the aisle where she was sitting, and said, "You know, Ellen, I'm not sure we should be so insistent on our rugged individualism. Maybe we should make some accommodations to China."

She glared at me. "I've been accommodating China all day. Now I'm doing what I want." There is no doubt that she is a person who is used to doing what she wants. I turned back to the scenes outside the bus, and thought about what it must be like for prisoners in her care.

As it turned out, though, enough people wanted to go into town to shop, so that after the bus took us back to the Guest House, it turned right around to take them to town. I didn't join them, not just because I really couldn't face another minute on the bus with American shoppers, but also because a reporter for the Baltimore Sun stationed in China was at the Guest House to visit Rich Friedman, a member of the Governor's Law Enforcement Commission in Maryland, and a very fine person. I can't remember the name of the reporter (it's written down somewhere), but I'm glad I stayed to hear him talk. What he had to tell the few of us who ventured to Rich's room to hear him was very interesting.

Only about half a dozen of us chose him over shopping, but that made it all the better. He talked about the difficulties of being in a foreign country with no government contacts. He talked about how difficult it had been to arrange to see a People's Court in action. It took him four months to arrange, producing a new skepticism in Aric and me about our own possibilities for such a visit.

But, most interesting of all, he spoke about crime in China. He is doing a story on crime, relying mainly on newspaper clippings he gets a friend to translate for him. He said that crime was definitely being viewed as a more and more serious problem here, though it doesn't begin to approach our own crime problem. He thinks that the strong sense of community and the crowded living conditions make constant citizen surveillance a fact of life, which greatly reduces the opportunities for committing crime. But he also noted that when the community rises up at a particularly offensive crime, it can have a powerful influence over the outcome.

He cited a case in a small town near Nanjing called Ma'anshan where a particularly heinous rape and murder was committed (is there any other kind?). The man was given the death sentence, but with a two-year reprieve, standard in such cases.

When "the people" heard of the brief reprieve, they "demonstrated their outrage." The court reversed itself, and the murderer was summarily executed. The Sun reporter told us that the story had actually appeared in the local newspaper, and urged us to ask the Nanjing Law School Faculty about it when we meet with them.

Before going to hear the journalist speak, we had some time to rest. Aric and I used the time to go for a walk. It was a very good walk outside the compound, a necessary escape from the regimentation of group travel. We went into a small, stark department store and a small market and looked around. We talked about the enormous egotism of all of us to have come to China believing that we were capable of winging it, unprepared and uncaring. We did not spare ourselves from this observation.

While walking, we passed a woman pushing her baby in a wonderful bamboo stroller. If I had the money, I would love to be able to bring one back to my benefactor, Naneen, who is expecting her first baby soon after we return.

While Mama buys vegetables, her baby waits in a bamboo stroller. After the newspaper man's talk, the bus returned with its load of shoppers and their cargo of loot, and we had about an hour to clean up before piling aboard the bus again for another feast. Although this multi-level restaurant did have a lot of Chinese patrons eating there, none was on our floor. I wonder who is being protected from whom. We had Peking duck, which — though I've actually had better in San Francisco — gave us the special thrill of having had Peking duck in Peking.

After dinner, when everyone else got back into the confines of the bus to go home to bed, Len Troppin and I decided to walk around. We talked about the state of the country and the world, his childhood in Brooklyn, mine in Ojai, and what it's like to work with a saint like Milt Rector, long the director of NCCD, and a giant in the field of criminal justice reform. My first impression of Len, this slightly stooped middle-aged man, was reinforced all along the way: he is truly a decent human being.

Though it was late, we saw wonderfully narrow Chinese streets with fruit vendors and open tailor shops. We wandered through Tienanmen Square, past the Mao Memorial and the Great Hall of the People, opposite the Gate of Heavenly Peace, which leads into The Forbidden City. We walked past smiling and unsmiling Chinese people, children playing on bicycles, families out for a walk, both the curious and the oblivious, the friendly and the not so friendly (very few). I was again transported back to the narrow Chinese streets of Tawau, where I lived for three years. There is something so Chinese that seems to transcend nationality, ideology and revolution, that calls forth such familiar feelings in me.

We walked and we talked. Finally, when we were both too tired to walk any more, we decided to try to get a taxi back to the Guest House. But how? Neither of us could remember how to get to the big Peace Hotel near the Guest House (which, according to Mr. Wong, had been built by the Soviets "when they were our friends"). So, we decided to cross the street to one of the ubiquitous kiosks on the corner, and ask the white uniformed security person inside (as opposed to the green uniformed People's Liberation Army soldiers outside — and most everywhere else) to get us a taxi.

After much mutually incomprehensible gesticulating, I remembered that I had the pass that Mr. Wong had written for me to get back past the security guards at the entrance to the Guest House. The note was passed around the gathering crowd of non-English speakers until, finally, another security person rode off on his bicycle to find us a cab. By that time, a strikingly handsome young Chinese man rode up on his bicycle and asked in flawless English, "Is there something the matter? Can I help you?" The help was already on its way.

Which brings me to a few general observations about this city and about our tour, before we set off tomorrow for Nanjing.

First, Peking is a most amazing place. We've been in this city of nine million people for four days, and not yet heard a siren! Bicycles are everywhere, and so is construction. Huge piles of bricks lay here and there, and whole parts of the city are either being torn down or built up. Where they get the capital for this massive construction remains a mystery. The Chinese seem to me so familiar, so much like my students in Malaysia. The kids play the same card games. Mr. Wong is comfortable enough with us to lose his temper — something I don't think I ever saw when I lived in Japan, at least not in front of *gai jin* — foreigners.

But there is something else, too, that you pick up almost by osmosis here. I don't know what to call it, exactly, except a strict but unwritten moral dictatorship, which would be smotheringly oppressive to me — and, I suspect, equally to a large number of Chinese who have failed to be "re-educated." Yet, clearly the education has worked well.

The most lasting impression I have, though, is that the Chinese are survivors. Their culture has survived famine and flood, imperialism and feudalism, civil war and World War. It will survive the current regime — whatever it happens to be or to become. I believe it will outlive the American culture, as we think of it, though that will not happen during my lifetime.

And what is our culture? Although I like almost everybody in this group individually, as a group we seem to turn into fat, rich and very callous Americans. We press candy and baubles on children who neither ask for nor seem to want them; we snap pictures by the million, and wave incessantly, like politicians running for office. And through it all, we genuinely believe we are, and by rights ought to be, loved for all this. Though Judge Bader-Mann offends me (and most everyone else) when he continually suggests that we can teach these poor benighted people everything we know, because, after all, we are the United States of America, to one degree or another, we are all Judge Bader-Manns.

Even recognizing the centuries-old resilience of this culture, my fear, honestly, is that we could, in legendary American style, innocence abroad, destroy the fabric, delicate as it is, woven out of an ancient culture and a new-born socialist government — by never realizing, or caring to realize, that we can love a people to death.

••••••••••••••••••••••••••••••••••••

Mr. Wong announced the sad news this morning that Madame Soong Ching Ling, the widow of Dr. Sun Yat Sen, had died yesterday, and that June 3 (my birthday) would be a national day of mourning when only commemorative activities will be allowed. All Chinese (one feels, without exception) will use that day to "commemorate Madame Sun" and without another word needing to be said. So different from us who take such perverse pleasure in not doing what we are told (or is that just me?). And yet, so similar to us in their lack of formality, their casual day-to-day interactions. It is a very difficult place to describe.

June 1, Arrival in Nanjing

When we arrived at the Beijing Airport this morning en route to Nanjing, I turned into an American chauvinist. As we walked toward the 727 jet, I thought, "What do these people know about flying an airplane... and especially a jet plane? I hope they aren't depending on revolutionary slogans to get this son-of-a-bitch off the ground..." I remember that my 7th grade social studies teacher, Mr. Brown, had once told the class that Chinese did not make good drivers because they had no experience with machinery. (I remember this because even at the time I recognized the claim as racial prejudice.) Now, twenty-five years later, egalitarianism was being put to the test. And in an airplane, yet, which, even under the best of circumstances (meaning, even at home), requires an act of faith on my part before boarding, knowing as I do, that this mechanical flying contraption defies the laws of god and man (not to mention woman).

After exchanging furtive looks of terror with Aric, I assumed a nonchalant pose, and mounted the ramp. When we entered the cabin, our worst fears were realized. First, the seats were closer together than anything you'd see on an American flight, even the super-duper savers. That made it difficult squeezing into your row, even if you had an aisle seat as I did, and virtually impossible to sit down without your knees touching your chin. Then there was the problem of hand-carried luggage — namely, where to put it. With almost no room in, around, or under the seats, people were stuffing flight bags, suitcases and briefcases into the overhead racks which were simple shelves about a foot wide that ran the length of both sides of the cabin. I wondered if the precariously-balanced load would make it even to the end of the runway. It did.

As the plane started to sprint down the runway before lift off —those few moments when my heart stops beating and my hands start sweating profusely enough to water a garden — I looked across the aisle from me where Aric was buckled in so tightly it looked like he had no waist at all. That was my salvation.

There he was, this kosher Jew from Brooklyn, eyes tightly shut, silently moving his lips in prayer. Forgetting that my life, too, depended on a successful take off, I watched Aric's lips move continuously until the plane had been airborne for some minutes. When he finally opened his eyes, I said, "Aric, I don't know what you were praying, but it obviously worked. Would you teach me?"

Relieved and smiling, he replied, "I won't teach you shit."

Then two stewardesses, dressed entirely in white, like nurses, came down the aisle carrying trays of hot tea. They were not pushing a handcart; they were balancing trays loaded with steaming hot cups of tea, and teetering down the aisle! As they passed me, I squinched myself up in anticipation of the plane lurching and me being scalded to death. Later, I gratefully accepted their offerings: hard candy, "China Pictorial" (a Chinese version of Life Magazine), and a pretty paper fan with a picture of a couple of cats on one side and an advertisement for CAAC, Civil Aviation Administration of China, on the other.

To our great relief — perhaps even surprise — we landed safely about an hour later.

The bus ride from the airport took us through the heart of this city of three million, and it is startlingly different from Beijing. The wide, sycamore-lined streets reminded me a little of the French colonial legacy in Saigon and Phnom Penh. Our local guide, Mr. Tsau, with his strong British accent, told us that 32 million sycamores, or plane trees as he and the English call them, have been planted since "liberation", and that 300,000 of them line the streets of Nanjing.

The bus ride ended on top of a little hill overlooking the city where our hotel is located. I suppose, after the *Diaoyutai*, anything else would look ordinary. And this hotel, built by the Australians, qualifies. It has a number of numbered buildings that resemble rectangular Quonset huts with yellow aluminum siding. Our rooms are simple — sort of a cross between an old motel room and a double at the YMCA. There are refrigerators, but alas, they are empty. The one amenity in each room is a large thermos filled with hot tea. So much for the life of luxury.

The activities planned here sound less frenzied, but equally enjoyable. We're going to the Friendship Store (something I've heard talked about by everyone I know who has ever been to China) for shopping, followed by a free evening. Tomorrow we'll start the day at the Sun Yat Sen memorial, followed by a visit to another law faculty, this time at Nanjing University. Then we'll have some local entertainment in the evening. On Wednesday morning, June 3, my birthday, we'll meet with a neighborhood mediation cadre in the morning and cruise the Yangtze River in the afternoon. Or, at least those with ten extra yuan for the boat ride will cruise the river.

I will not be among them. It is not the extra yuan that will prevent me from joining the others (though I do resent any added costs after what we have been soaked for this tour). I'm acting on the premise that you've seen one river boat cruise you've seen 'em all — as well as the certainty that everyone else will be on board the boat, giving me the opportunity to wander alone, and contemplate life at 38.

I'll have to stop here for a while... group lunch time!

Friendship Store, Department Store

We did nothing but shop this afternoon, which was fine — except for the fact that the Friendship Store is another one of those places, like the hotel we are staying at and the restaurants we eat at, where ordinary Chinese are forbidden to enter. I bought myself a Mao jacket and hat (and Karamoko bought me a red star to sew on it, which I did), as well as a few little things for a few little people. The thing I need the most, though — film — I could not find. (I have one of those $8 Kodak cameras, the kind that used to be called "brownies".) It requires 110 film. I'm hoping it's available somewhere else on the tour, perhaps tomorrow at the Memorial. The tour book was right about one thing: take half as many clothes as you think you'll need and twice as much film. Unfortunately, I didn't read the tour book until this morning.

Unlike Beijing where our presence hardly created a stir, Nanjing-ites seem much less familiar with us *fung mau kui* — red-headed devils. We draw huge crowds wherever we go, singly, in groups, and even on the bus. We walked through several multi-floored Chinese department stores today (we are free to enter "their" stores and restaurants, they are just not free to enter "ours"), and I could always find one of us by locating the crowd. I was never wrong.

I watched from the third floor balcony, in fact, as our Boston Brahman, Pebble the Prosecutor, stood behind a counter on the floor below actually trying on different sizes of pants for her Mao suit. She drew a huge crowd — just as she would have done had she decided to try on pants in the middle of Penny's. I think there's something about being in a foreign country that makes us feel invisible.

Aric's wife's niece's sister's cousin, or something like that, has been a student here for two years. Tomorrow, after our law school visit, Aric has invited me to join them to do "whatever it is you do in Nanjing."

Tonight the group seemed much more acceptable to me. Perhaps I'm just turning into one of them — or accepting the fact that I always have been. In fact, I think we've all come to accept each other a little more. The things that offended me the most, like talking down to the Chinese, offering candy and Polaroid pictures, and thinking we're important because people flock around us, are still happening, but either I am getting used to them, or the initial shock of being here in China and surrounded by Chinese — a first for everybody — is wearing off a little.

It's sometimes difficult for me to remember that most of my own prejudices about the Chinese were dispelled only by my earlier exposure to their culture. Ignorance is responsible for prejudice. Kay told me, for example, that until this trip, she had never thought of Chinese men as handsome. Now, having been here for less than a week, she thinks many of them (like Mr. Wong, for example) are downright sexy.

Now, if you'll excuse me, I'm taking this sexy non-Chinese to bed. Good-bye Beijing; hello Nanjing.

June 2, Dr. Sun Yat Sen Memorial and the Death of his widow, Madame Soong Ching-Ling, Nanjing

This morning, after a breakfast of thousand-year-old eggs, cucumber and chicken, pickled radish and congee (Chinese rice porridge) — a Chinese feast for me, spurned by almost everybody else in the group, who ate scrambled eggs and toast — we set out for Dr. Sun Yat Sen's Memorial, east of the city.

As we neared the East Wall (Nanjing is surrounded by an ancient wall, constructed some time during the Ming Dynasty when Nanjing was established as the nation's capital), we passed by the former headquarters of Chiang Kai-shek's Kuomintang, now the headquarters of the Provisional Government of the People's Republic. It is a place of especial importance in China's recent history, being the spot where, in 1912, delegates elected Dr. Sun as the first President of the Republic, and then ratified the new constitution. It is also the spot Chiang had to evacuate in 1938 as the Imperial Japanese forces moved in and began what is referred to as "the rape of Nanjing" in which many hundreds of thousands of Chinese men were killed, and Chinese women raped.

Sun Yat Sen Memorial, Nanjing

This morning, a large crowd of Chinese stood solemnly opposite the gate as an ancient movie camera whirred away. Untypically, no explanation was offered, but I'm sure it is related to the death of Madame Sun, who is to be buried tomorrow, a day of national mourning. In fact, I forgot to mention that yesterday, on our way from the Guest House to the Beijing Airport, we passed by Tiananmen Square, which was alive with people — over a million, the paper said — waiting to view her body inside the Great Hall of the People.

The Sun Memorial itself is an imposing structure at the top of a long, and very wide flight of steps. From the top, you can see a magnificent panorama of forested lushness — the view that persuaded Dr. Sun to choose this place for his final rest, rather than his birthplace, Canton.

The Memorial is in a large park, which is obviously very popular with the Chinese. Of the thousands there, my favorite was a little girl, perhaps four years old, who posed for the American and European photographers that kept pouring out of buses. She was wearing the uniform of the People's Liberation Army (PLA) — green pants and jacket, with red cloth bars on the collar, and a green cap with a red star just above the peak.

Little girl in uniform of People's Liberation Army (PLA) on steps of
the Sun Yat Sen Memorial

From the parking lot at the bottom of the hill, you can look up to
the Memorial through a splendid triple-arched, four-pillared gate. The
whole thing is topped with glittering blue tile, like the roof of the
mausoleum itself. Climbing up those steps (and climbing, and
climbing), you pass huge bronze urns and bronze animals, cranes and
turtles, and elaborate pagoda-like bronzes with multi-tiered roofs.
Inside the dark, cool and calming mausoleum, are the actual remains

of Dr. Sun in a coffin that lies in front of a huge, marble statue of the seated Sun Yat Sen, like a Chinese Lincoln Memorial.

After coming down from the hill, we walked around the park. I loved the huge stone turtles that were hidden among the trees, and I climbed a nine-story pagoda. But my favorite building was a gigantic structure, a Buddhist temple called the Beamless Hall. Made entirely of bricks, its gracefully arched doorway and arching windows allowed light to stream into its cavernous chambers in brilliant patterns that were endlessly changing. In the middle of one of the rooms was a huge stage. For some reason, few people seemed to share my enthusiasm for the great building, and I found myself in glorious solitude for many minutes. (Solitude seldom gets measured in more than seconds here.)

We returned to the hotel for lunch, and, in a short while, we'll be going to the Nanjing University law school, where, we are told, no students are enrolled at this time (an administrator's dream). Apparently, the law school has only recently been re-established after having been closed down during the Cultural Revolution. After our meeting, Aric, his roommate, Greenhaven prison warden Carl Berry, and I will visit Aric's wife's relative or friend who has been studying here in China for two years. That should be interesting.

When we woke up this morning, my own roommate, Doug McDonald had stomach cramps and the runs (Chiang Kai-shek's revenge?), and a black tongue! Not, we are told by Bill Josephson who knows everything, the first stages of bubonic plague, but your common, run-of-the-mill, ordinary, garden variety trots. As Bill said, "It will pass." I only hope it doesn't pass to me.

....

University Student and the Cultural Revolution

This afternoon and evening were full and fine. We went to Nanjing University for the scheduled meeting with the law faculty, and when we entered the room, there was the long table we have become familiar with, the faculty sitting on one side and empty chairs for us on the other, as well as the ever-present tea mugs at each setting. What made this visit particularly satisfying to me was the large number of students sitting away from the table, along the walls. These students, we were told, are English language students eager to listen to native speakers and to practice their English. They offered to take anyone who was interested around the campus, one-on-one, while the meeting went on. Immediately, about half the group stood to take the campus stroll, including Kay and me.

Aric told me later that what I missed at the meeting was an embarrassing step-by-step description of the U.S. criminal justice system, from arrest to imprisonment, that took thirty minutes to get through, and ended with the lecturer (foundation grantee evaluator, attorney Steve Kelban) asking, "How does this differ from your system?" To which the erudite professors, not missing a beat, returned the question by asking how the British law governing pre-trial detention differed from ours — a question that went unanswered.

But even if their meeting had been full of important information, I could not possibly have learned as much as I did spending an hour with my eighteen-year old student, Wu Jang Ming.

He told me what it had been like, as a nine-year-old child, to be banished to the countryside to work on the land during the Cultural Revolution. (His parents were both teachers, the most visible targets for the youthful Red Guard to attack.) There was little food, and it was very difficult for his parents, though he didn't suffer as much as they.

He said that the worst part of it for people his age was that education was virtually non-existent. Although schools continued to operate for that generation, the teachers were barely high school graduates themselves since professional teachers were banished from the classrooms. What they taught was often wrong. He remembered, for example, opening a book with a picture of the Mississippi River, flowing from north to south. He approached his teacher and asked him why the rivers in America flowed from north to south when those in China flow from west to east. "My teacher looked at me with a pair of startled eyes, and said, 'That is because there are mountains in the north and plains in the south.'" Jang Ming didn't think this could be the real reason, but had no books or other resources to consult. (His fascination with the Mississippi continues to this day, and I have promised to send him some picture books.)

He said he thought the reason for the Cultural Revolution was Chairman Mao's fear of being regarded as Stalin was, after people learned of his excesses. To alter that historical perspective, he freed the youth to do what they wanted, and it quickly got out of control. (Can you imagine the consequences of American high school students turned loose to pursue their animosities toward authority figures, in general, and teachers in particular?) Bands of young people roamed the countryside "punishing the bourgeoisie," sometimes killing them and sometimes just beating them up. About this he added, "Chairman Mao made a mistake, but he was still a very great man. He gave us the Communist Party!"

Quite by accident, I learned that this egalitarian society is still steeped in sexism. I asked Jang Ming why there seemed to be so many male students and an even greater proportion of male teachers if, as we are told, admission is based solely on the results of matriculation exams. He replied without a moment's hesitation that boys are smarter than girls. No amount of argument would shake him from this belief.

After the campus tour, we walked back to the meeting, which was still going on. During the question and answer period that followed, I was called on by Dinni to answer one of the professor's questions about our use of the death penalty. (Her calling on me was not only a direct result of our earlier decision to provide an alternative view, but also because I am more fluent with the status of capital punishment than anyone else on the tour, and certainly more vocal about it. It probably didn't hurt that I was wearing my bright red T-shirt with the little electric chairs all over it and the command: Stop The Death Penalty.)

During my answer, which went into a little of the judicial history of the death penalty before explaining its current status and the fact that over 800 people are awaiting execution in America, one could hear Judge B.M. muttering under his breath. When I finally briefly delved into the organized opposition to capital punishment, the judge's mutterings became a loud, articulated point of view. "Not everyone agrees with that," he exploded. That's not my view... Some of us think more people should be sentenced to death..." What a putz!

The really sad thing is that I got the distinct impression that the law professors, like the Justice Ministers in Beijing, pressed us for details on the death penalty and its use in the United States not as ammunition against the decadent West, but to apply it more widely in China. The number of crimes (including desertion from the army) for which the new code provides the death penalty is growing.

Then I remembered what the Baltimore Sun reporter had told us of the capital trial in Ma'anshan, and I asked what they knew about it. I explained what we had been told, that the two-year reprieve had apparently been reversed when "the masses" objected, and the defendant was summarily executed. There followed a long and volatile exchange among the Chinese faculty, which finally got translated simply as, "That did not happen. The man was executed, but according to the law." It is impossible to tell what made them so excited at my question, but my guess is that I had asked something they had not spoken of in their formal presentation — something which I should not know about. But whatever it was, the question caused quite a stir — much yelling and gesticulating and talking back and forth in Chinese. Another of those times that I regretted not having taken up Mandarin.

Immediately after the meeting, I made my way to the student who had served as interpreter. He had an amazing command of both English vocabulary and pronunciation. In fact, considering that none of the students had ever been in an English-speaking environment, all were very impressive. Anyway, as we walked out of the building and back toward the bus (though Aric and Carl and I were not going to reboard the bus, mercifully), I asked him the same question I had put to my guide earlier about the disproportionate number of men in both the faculty and the student body. He answered by saying that men are more studious than women. I couldn't resist asking him if he thought that was a genetic distinction. He paused, let the question percolate for a moment, and said, "No, of course not. This must be related to our feudal past. We must work on this problem."

What startled me most about this exchange was not that sexism still exists in China. After my three years with the Chinese in Malaysia, I would have been dumbfounded if it did not. What startled me most was that there is apparently no revolutionary slogan to deal with the sexism of the past (and, of course, the present). Or, if there are such slogans, they weren't familiar to either of the two students I had talked to. Now that I think about it, I have heard the slogan "Women hold up half of the sky," but only from the American women on this tour. That is, after we climbed the Great Wall, I remember my "dear friend" Ellen, the keeper of jailed women in New York City, proudly repeating the slogan. I think I first heard it in a documentary about China put together by Shirley MacLaine and her all-woman TV crew, during their fantastic China tour. So, I assume, she heard the slogan from Chinese. At any rate, even if the student had no slogan to fit a particular sin —

in this case, sexism — he was able to fall back on a sort of Golden Rule slogan to fit all occasions ("This must be related to our feudal past.")

Mother and daughter in Nanjing

Our evening with the American students was more wonderful than I had foreseen. First, Aric's wife's friend's sister, Katy, who lives in a dorm on campus, took us by city bus (our first experience with inner-city public transportation) to a wonderful little Hunan restaurant where, unlike any other place we have visited to date, we were the only foreigners. We had hot spicy fish, spicy pork, a delicious soup and fried vegetables. It was a "pure" Chinese eating establishment, like those I knew so well in that small Malaysian town of Tawau — noisy, dirty, alive. There were perhaps ten round tables in the dining room. At the table next to us was a family with their two small children. They couldn't take their eyes off us (the kids, that is), and we couldn't take ours off them. Their mother continually scolded, "*Sit fan, sit fan*" — eat your dinner!

After dinner, instead of taking the bus, we decided to walk back to the dorm. We strolled along the streets, alive with people on foot and on bicycles. When we got to the dorm, we went to Katy's small room, which she shares with two other Americans and a Chinese student. There, with Katy and two other Americans who have been studying Chinese history, culture and language at the university for two years, we heard the most amazing stories.

For instance, about a year ago, they were invited to attend a murder trial in town, which they did. The accused was found guilty, sentenced to death, and taken in the back of a pick-up truck, with his head shaved, to the local sports field. According to one of the students, the *coup de grace* — a bullet behind the ear — was administered in front of live television cameras!

They spoke about the general feeling of terrible isolation (the same complaint we heard from the Baltimore Sun correspondent in Beijing), and their inability to learn about events taking place in China. Often, they said, their best source of information were clippings sent from home about China. Sometimes, they said, they hear about neighborhood events only months after they occur. Yet, clearly, they love the people, the food, the adventure and the newness of the experience. They love China.

They told us that the problem of juvenile delinquency, which we hear so much about in the States, is what we would describe as petty harassment of older people, and vandalism by street gangs. But, belying popular Chinese slogans to the contrary, "the masses" do not rise up as one to reprimand the young and set them on the right path. Instead, they are cowed and submissive. The students spoke of beggars still existing, and they wondered what happens to the vast majority of

Chinese who do not live in cities, who do not even live on the rail line. They have heard that feudalism is still the law of much of that land, that the powerful few still control the powerless many, and that it is still a matter of who you know and not what you know or what you have done that counts. What is life like for those hundreds of millions, they wondered. And so do I.

I envied them their time here, time to absorb some of the myriad impressions that seem to bombard you constantly. I asked about the possibilities for teaching here, and was told that the foreign "experts" (native English speakers) had their own, rather plush housing, and were paid about 600 yuan a month, five or six times what their Chinese counterparts are paid. That's not exactly the kind of arrangement I had in mind. I wonder if there are any foreign teachers at the high school level?

When we got back to the hotel, it was too early to go to bed, so I went up to the "disco club" on the second floor of another building in the complex. To my surprise, none of our group was there, but there was a group of young Japanese tourists. I said hello to them, and they replied with typical Japanese flattery, telling me how clever I was to speak Japanese. They invited me to sit and drink with them, but before I could summon two complete sentences from the dim recesses of my memory (*Gomenasai, watakushi-wa Nihongo-o hanasei-nai* — So sorry, I don't speak Japanese), a loud group of Americans poured into the small room. It was us.

I was immediately whisked away by the likes of Lynn Zeller, Pebble, Karamoko, Jon Bowman (the silent one whose look-alike travel companion, Ann, is not his wife, rumor has it), Jim Galvin, the NCCD statistician, and dear Kay. To varying degrees (varying from dizzy to dazed), they were all as drunk as skunks, to coin a phrase. The room, which was permanently decorated in a crepe-paper Christmas motif, was immediately taken over by the Americans. Lynn commandeered the stereo and found as many oldies-but-not-such-goodies as she could, and played them over and over. Those that we knew, we sang. Those that we didn't know, we also sang. There was a small, deserted dance floor, which we immediately occupied, like a conquering army. The floor is made of wooden tiles about the size of Scrabble letters. As we shimmied and shook during repeated playings of bad music, these tiles began coming loose.

Karamoko, who was, surprisingly, not the most rambunctious among us, tore his tight white pants right down the back, and had to make a quick exit. From the expressions on their faces, it was obvious that the Chinese in the room disapproved of our bizarre behavior — and I am not talking about the fact that shy and retiring Jon turns into a veritable Cassanova when he is drunk, kissing everyone in sight, including me and Karamoko, or that we danced as couples, triples, quadruples and singles (my specialty). No, what I think disturbed them most was that when they finally turned the lights to bright, pointedly suggesting that it was time to pack it in, the wood floor, which had had one loose tile when we began, was a shambles when we were done. Only a few tiles remained intact.

In the corner of the room, half a dozen Chinese men sat engrossed in a MahJongg game. They seemed completely oblivious to us, adding only the steady click clacking of Mah-Jongg tiles to the din as our activities grew progressively more raucous.

I wonder what grand conclusions our Chinese audience drew about the decadent West — or whether, instead, they envied our freedom.

June 3, Nanjing Mediation Committee

"Happy birthday to you, happy birthday to you, happy birthday dear Michael..." That's how the group greeted me this morning as they waited for the dining room doors to open for our morning feed. I had just returned from my morning walk, a wonderful constitutional taken with Bill Josephson around the back streets at the bottom of the hill from the hotel. We saw people standing in doorways brushing their teeth, men and women selling fried bread surrounded by clamoring customers, including dozens of beautifully braided girls and smiling boys carrying books on their way to elementary school. In front of one house, a man and young woman, probably father and daughter, sat at a table making a rug. Around the corner, an entire dirt road had been converted into an open market, with hawkers selling vegetables, eggs, chickens, ducks and bread.

Father and daughter making a rug in their doorway, Nanjing

At the end of one street was an entrance to some kind of barracks. It had two red pillars on either side, with writing on them, and an army-green arch connecting them. In the middle of the arch, the Red Flag hung motionless. There, for the first time, we were turned away.

As usual here in Nanjing, the presence of two tall, white foreigners created quite a stir. Crowds gathered wherever we went. I'm getting used to it.

After breakfast, we went to a neighborhood mediation committee. As the bus pulled into the courtyard, the neighborhood committee members stood to applaud us. It is the same greeting we got from the prison administration and guards, the same as from the law school faculty and English language students. When we leave, they stand again and applaud. I fear we're beginning to think it's our due.

The setting for the presentation was lovely. Wooden houses, from which an occasional face peers out, surrounded a square courtyard graced with swaying sycamore trees. At the far end was a raised wooden stage. Tables were arranged in a rectangle on the stage. Behind the long table sat members of the mediation committee, and we were ushered onto the stage to sit facing them, with our backs to the neighborhood people who sat in folding chairs in the courtyard below. Each of us had a covered porcelain mug, which was continually refilled with hot tea by attentive and attractive young women. After being officially welcomed by the director of the neighborhood committee, Mr. Liu, we were briefed by his assistant, Ms. Fu, who reminded me of Mao's widow, Chiang Ching, both in looks and in her forceful presentation.

Although I took copious notes, pages of them, the basic message was that mediation is a way of preventing disputes from escalating into criminal matters, a way of educating the grassroots about the law, and a way of reconciling people who must live in close proximity. Since people live so close together, disputes are usually brought to the attention of the committee very early in the process. Although it makes me fidget uncomfortably to think of my neighbors always aware of disputes-in-the-making, for a country of over a billion people, I doubt if there's any other way to deal with this reality. And even in a country of "only" two hundred million or so, I don't doubt that we would be far better off with more mediation and less criminal prosecution. Still, as she talked, I wondered if it were possible to keep secrets here, to maintain what we rugged individuals like to describe as a "private life."

According to Ms. Fu, the mediation committees play a very important role for Chinese young people, disrupted by the suspension of schooling during the Cultural Revolution, and therefore in need of special nurturing and care, "to turn them from the bad path." Judging from what we were told, the committees have a good deal of success, despite having no power to impose solutions, no power to coerce behavior, and no power to punish violators.

We heard countless, seemingly endless examples of successful mediation efforts.

For example, one couple who wanted another child after having two daughters (they wanted a son) were not only "made to understand" that boys and girls are equal, but that by having more children, they were undermining the national policy of birth control. (That policy, by the way, is spoken about everywhere, and advertised on billboards. A short time ago, the slogan was "One is best; two is most." The new slogan is "None is best; one is most.") In another case, which began as a fight between children of different families and soon escalated into a family feud, the adults were "made to understand" that the children had originally fought "owing to the influence of the Gang of Four," and that they should stop their quarreling.

But my favorite case was that of a city girl who fell in love with a man from the country. Because of that, her mother opposed the match, while her father supported his daughter. "We explained that it was wrong for parents to meddle," explained the meddling committee, "and also that the young should respect their parents." With this explanation, apparently, the mother stopped meddling and the daughter "exercised patience." In time, the mother supported her daughter, the young couple was married, and everyone lived happily ever after.

After the Committee meeting, we returned to the hotel for lunch, and then went off to cruise the Yangtze (the river Chairman Mao famously swam when he was an old man). Although I had determined not to go on that boat ride, my decision was not well received by our local guide, the officious Mr. Tsau. Apparently fearing that, left alone, I would get myself (and, by extension, himself) into trouble, he kept insisting that I must join the group on the boat. Perhaps he was motivated by my pauper's disclaimer (though I wouldn't have gone on the river cruise even if I had the ten yuan to squander), because he said that I didn't have to pay, presumably because Lynn Zeller, who had already paid, was indisposed, and remained in her hotel room.

When we got down to the wharf, Mr. Tsau actually pulled me along by hand until we were the last two people yet to board the tug-like vessel. He stepped aboard, pulling me along, but I gave a sharp tug and pulled away — a brazen act of rugged individualism. As the boat left the dock, I winked at Mr. Tsau, who had a stricken look on his face. Then I turned away and wandered back up the river bank.

A number of fishing boats lying low in the water were just setting out for their afternoon catch. I stood on the bridge connecting the shore to the wharf, and waved to the fisher people passing below me. In the back of the boats, a man or woman stood with a foot on the tiller. In the front, another man stood, readying a large fishing net, which he then cast repeatedly into the river, hauling in a few fish at a time. All on board wore hats, usually those Chinese hats that rise to a point on top as protection against the strong sun.

Smiling at me on a bridge over the Yangtze, a fisherman rows his boat.
I walked through a residential neighborhood next to the river and
down to the giant bridge which spans it — and which is depicted
on the two-yuan note. This bridge is a technological masterpiece, an
accomplishment that, we were told, stymied the Russian technicians
who once served as "advisors" in China, and is, therefore, a source of
tremendous pride to the Chinese who succeeded where the Russians
had failed. It is a very impressive thing to behold, a gigantic steel bridge
nearly a mile long, with automobile and bus traffic on the top deck and
train traffic on the lower one. From the base of a huge pillar, I looked
up, past the red flag flying at half staff, to a huge stone statue honoring

the laborers who had performed this amazing feat of construction. I walked into an exhibition hall at the base of the bridge where another huge, stone Chairman Mao greets you. Unlike the solemn-faced Mao that surveys the campus at Beijing University, this giant Mao stands with his right arm raised in permanent salutation, a faint smile on his marble lips.

The red flag flies at half staff to honor widow of Dr. Sun Yat Sen, Madame Soong Ching-Ling, who died on May 29. Note the Monument to the People atop this pride-producing bridge spanning the Yangtze River.

As I walked back along the river to the dock, I saw a wonderful little vignette acted out right before my eyes. About a dozen young boys, maybe ten or eleven years old, were being yelled at for some infraction by a uniformed PLA soldier. He was not much more than a boy, himself, though an automatic rifle swung ominously from his shoulder. Whatever it was the kids had done, he was mad as hell. The boys stood before him silently, their little heads down, while his tongue-lashing grew more and more agitated. Then, from way down the road, a couple of teenage girls yelled something at him. He yelled back. They yelled again, and he angrily moved in their direction. As he did, the kids said something among themselves in hushed tones, and immediately ran off in the opposite direction, brushing against me as they ran past. By the time the young soldier realized what was happening and came running in hot pursuit, they were long-since out of sight.

The uplifting thing about the incident was not just that it happened, this time-honored tradition of razzing authority, but that the few adults looking on were clearly rooting for the kids. When the soldier looked away, they exchanged the furtive smiles of conspirators. When he faced them, they gazed out at the river, a look of studied indifference on their faces.

Buying potatoes, street market, Nanjing

When the Gang of Thirty returned, we went to the Nanjing Zoo where the giant panda entertained most everybody all afternoon. (Coming from D.C., where the National Zoo has two giant pandas on loan from the government of China, Kay and I did not get nearly as engrossed in the critter as the others did.) Aric shot three rolls of film of the non-bear, a complete ham that kept circling his cage, always turning a somersault at precisely the same spot. I was perversely pleased with Polaroid Bob's perfect photos... of the wire fence surrounding the enclosure. His camera, the latest model, automatically focuses on the nearest object. Unfortunately, it does not have the capacity to ignore the occasional object that might come between you and what you're shooting. So, his photos, taken in quick succession, miss the panda altogether, but reveal the inter-locking wire fencing in vivid detail. I say this gave me perverse pleasure (indeed, it seemed to give everybody a good laugh, most especially Bob himself) because of what the Polaroid camera has come to symbolize for me on this trip.

Every time a child comes within eye-shot, out come the Polaroids. We snap the shutters incessantly. Coupled with this display of our benign and friendly techno-logical superiority is the habit of a number of people on this tour to raise their arms, as if by instinct, to wave from the bus wherever we happen to be. It is almost as if they believe that the Chinese who have been so graced will treasure the moment forever, endlessly regaling their friends and relatives with stories of how the great white fathers and mothers blessed them with a regal wave — a magical moment to be passed down from generation to generation.

Am I too cynical? I suppose so, but I remember the pictures of Hawaii in the early days of contact with the mainland, when rich American tourists threw coins into the water for the happy natives to dive for. And I also remember what has become of the happy natives... Besides, the American students told us that the Polaroid has made their lives miserable because everywhere they go, crowds of Chinese follow them begging to have their Polaroids taken, despite the fact that most of the students carry only conventional cameras. This has happened to us, too, so I understand their complaint, and sympathize.

We're back at the hotel now, and will soon be eating. From this morning's greeting, I am prepared for a surprise dinner in my honor. If called on to make a speech, I will say that as for birthday speeches, none is best and one is most. Or that, although I have improved with each passing year, there is much to be desired and I will try harder (a constant Chinese refrain). Or that, of my 38 birthdays, six have been spent in Asia, each more memorable than the last. (That final assertion is not true, of course, but I may say it anyway.)

Or, maybe I'll just say thank you.

••••••••••••••••••••••••••••••••••••

We Celebrate My 38th

Dinner is over and it was actually a very fine one. We had shad, the specialty of this hotel, and chocolate mousse for dessert. (Even though it wasn't the best mousse I've ever eaten, I had three at dinner and took one back to my room for a midnight snack... no question about which of the deadly sins is my favorite.) I received various toasts, including a serious one from ex-prisoner Karamoko who told the assembled throng that of all of us, he respected only the work of Kay and me, an observation guaranteed to win me friends and influence me people.

While this was going on, a Japanese tour group at the other end of the dining room, realizing that there was a birthday celebration in progress, deputized one of their members to come over and also offer me a toast. Having gulped down *maotai* with each succeeding toast, I couldn't resist trying to say something in Japanese. I stood up, rather uncertainly, and began to say, in Japanese, that my friends wanted me to say something in Japanese, but that I had forgotten how. Unfortunately, the forgetting part was the operative phrase. All I could get out was "*Watakushi-no tomodachi-wa... Watakushi-no tomodachi-wa...*" — My friends... My friends... I just couldn't remember how to say "want" in Japanese. It didn't matter much, anyway, since only the Japanese knew I couldn't complete the sentence. As far as my traveling companions were concerned, I was fluent in Japanese.

My only regret about the merriment, which went on in various rooms after dinner, was that Mr. Wong could not join in. Earlier in the day, at lunch, he had made sure that I got a plate of "longevity noodles," a traditional birthday dish among the Chinese. (Longevity noodles look and taste uncannily like ordinary, short-lived noodles...) But tonight, he sat alone in his room, watching the funeral ceremonies of Madame Sun on television. The day had been declared a day of mourning, during which there was to be no drinking or partying — a declaration we blithely ignored.

Mr. Wong watched the solemn events all evening long, as we went in to pay our respects, individually or in groups of two or three.

June 4, En route to Wuxi

We are on a luxuriously comfortable East German train, bound for Wuxi, China. I feel that this day is going to be wonderful, despite a sour, inauspicious beginning.

Pebble, who is always the last to arrive at the bus, the last to arrive at meals, the last to return from shopping ("If Pebble's here, everybody's here," someone always says when she arrives), apparently was packing furiously this morning at the last minute. One of the amenities each room has is a beautiful thermos filled with hot tea, and in her hurry, she knocked over the one in her room, breaking it (which, she says, she didn't realize). She finished packing and left the room. Before she could get to the bus, however, the Chinese maid came running after her demanding that she pay for the broken thermos. It cost 16 yuan — about $12. Pebble, the D.A., was outraged. By the time she finished revving up, she was screaming, "They're lucky I don't sue them for putting a broken thermos in my room!" She had apparently completely forgotten having said at the onset of her tantrum that "it might have broken when it tipped over."

Mr. Wong was called on to mediate the dispute. He tried to speed the conclusion, since the rest of us were waiting on the bus to go to the train station. Pebble obstinately refused to concede anything, arguing like the prosecutor she is — or, more likely, the spoiled rich kid she is. It was finally resolved when Pebble very grudgingly accepted a compromise: she magnanimously agreed to pay half the value of the thermos. She maintained an air of righteous indignation all the way to the train station, pretending to be the injured party who had, nevertheless, agreed to the unfair compromise because she is such a gracious person.

That she refused to pay for what she broke is outrageous. That she yelled at Mr. Wong during the fracas is intolerable. My guess is that he ended up paying the other 8 yuan, saving the hotel maid from having to pay what amounts to one quarter of her monthly salary. What privileged arrogance to have threatened to sue a hotel maid in China for what Pebble herself undoubtedly broke.

I banished all my ugly thoughts as soon as we entered the train. With its wide aisles and curtained windows, it is nicer than any train I've been on in America or Europe. Uniformed stewardesses — always female — continually pass through the coach with hot tea. Train travel is so much more civilized than air travel.

I have just had a wonderful conversation with Mr. Wong, whom I chose to sit next to. We spoke about China, the Revolution, the people. He said he thought it was a good sign that people like Mao were judged by human standards. Elevating him to the position of a god, making him infallible, demeans the people who are, in fact, responsible for building and maintaining a nation. Like the young Chinese student who took me around Nanjing University, Mr. Wong acknowledged that Mao was a great man who, "like all people, made mistakes."

I asked him if he wasn't a little worried about the inordinate attention that is heaped on us, the first-class treatment we are always accorded, the fact that certain places, like the Friendship Stores and our hotels, are reserved for "us" only as in the days of overt imperialism. He agreed that this was a problem, but said he thought it would be impossible for us to live in the same conditions as the Chinese now live, considering their poverty. He thinks that as the economic conditions of the people rise, these problems will disappear. But when he spoke of the great deference paid to foreigners, a fleeting expression of anger flashed in his eyes. He said many Chinese have spoken of the problem of being kept out of places, as if they might contaminate the spots reserved for the "colonialists." He said, "You have asked a very important question."

And I resolve never to enter another Friendship Store.

June 4, Arrival in Wuxi

Oh, what an enchanting place! I think I have found the Chinese spot for my spirit's rest — though I'm not ready to lay it down yet. We wandered along one of the canals that crisscross the ancient city of less than a million people, like Venice, and were surrounded by people everywhere, smiling, laughing, touching. Not even the children seemed shy, as this troop of Americans swept down the crowded street next to the canal taking pictures of everything in sight.

A beautiful old man with sparse whiskers stood in his doorway, and waved tentatively, gently. A woman sold *char siu bau* — the pork buns that were my breakfast every morning for three years when I lived in Malaysian Borneo. I immediately got in line to buy one, the first in the group to ignore People-to-People's "better safe-than-sorry" warnings about eating food from street vendors. When I got to the window of her stall, I could remember how to ask how much it cost (*Do sao chien?*) but I couldn't remember enough to understand her answer. I gave her a one-yuan note, which she returned with the *bau*. I protested, but to no avail. She refused my money while insisting that I take the pork bun, which — surprise, surprise — I did.

Old man watches from his doorway

It was delicious. The throng of Chinese onlookers, especially the younger ones, watched me eating, amused. Mr. Wong later told me that the price for the bun is ten *fen* — less than a dime — and that she would probably have to pay for what I had eaten.

While most of us explored, a handful — 8 or 10 of the not-so-spry members of the group — stood at the top of the bridge that arches gracefully over the canal, handing out balloons to the children, pencils to the adults, handfuls of candy, and — need I say it? — Polaroid pictures by the gross, like self-imagined John D. Rockefellers striding through the streets of New York. Actually, the sight of Art Lane, a 6'6" retired Federal judge and Ronald Reagan look-alike (as described by one of the hotel waiters in Nanjing) clad in Bermuda shorts, a T-shirt and a Mao cap with red star sewn on was hilarious. There he stood, with several others from the bus, surrounded by so many Chinese that the bridge was totally impassable, towering above everybody, and waving with both arms like a man running for President. God love us.

Earlier that morning, we toured a silk factory. Actually, only half of us toured the factory. The other half went to the Friendship Store to shop.

The factory tour was a fascinating one that began with a discussion of silk farming (we will visit a nearby silk farm tomorrow). We were led through the various processes involved in spinning the silk as we were led through rows and rows of women pulling invisible strands of silk out of the air and twisting them together with other invisible strands, until a visible thread could be discerned even by our eyes. We discussed the factory mediation process, there being a mediation committee in every factory. Then we visited the factory's nursery, which held some of the most beautiful babies we've seen so far, each in an individual octagonal playpen made of bamboo. And finally, we were led into the outdoor courtyard with a million posters extolling the virtues of safety and hard work.

During the now-familiar briefing following the tour, I asked Ms. Wu, the factory manager, why there were so many women employed, and whether the proportion of women in the work force was the same as the proportion of women managers. Despite having already been shocked in Nanjing by the sexist beliefs of students, I was now shocked again by her answer: 80% of the workers are women "because women's hands are more delicate than men's," and, therefore, "they are better equipped to work there than men."

Apparently, men are born with better management skills than women, though, because only 40% of the managers are women. Pearl West correctly pointed out that this is a far higher proportion of women managers than you would find in any American enterprise, but that still does not offset my disappointment that sexism remains so pervasive. I guess I had thought its most blatant manifestations would be a thing of the past, like binding women's feet. In fact, there is a strange mixture of the feudal past and the revolutionary present; the female head of a factory explaining that women have better hands for weaving silk than men.

After the factory tour, we took the walk along the canal that I already told you about, then back to the hotel for lunch. After lunch, free time. Many people took taxis back into town, but I wandered around the grounds of this huge hotel, which is outside of town on a large lake called the *Taihu*. (*Tai* means big in Chinese, as in *tai fun* — typhoon — which translates literally as big wind.) It is beautiful. There are small gardens all around it that I happened on quite by accident. I came across two teenagers hunting for birds' eggs in the eaves of a small, square shrine right on the water's edge behind the hotel. They had taken off their shoes, and, while one crouched, the other climbed on his shoulders and felt around under the eaves above him. Teamwork. Old people sat along the lakeshore fishing. Lovers strolled the gardens.

Now, we are about to leave again for the city. There is another offering of local entertainment, another Chinese opera. Aric and I have decided to go into town on the bus with the others, but to slip away for a walk before the opera begins. We have had such little time for aimless walking, and both of us are looking forward to it.

It's amazing that we can still walk, with the amount of food we have been putting away, almost non stop. We've just finished another huge Chinese feast. Even though I starved myself for a month before this trip so that I could eat like a pig, I'm beginning to resemble one.

•••

A walk with Aric in the park

Instead of attending the opera, Aric and I walked for hours tonight along the canal that ended in a lovers' lane. There were couples strolling, sitting on benches, sitting on the canal wall, talking, laughing, kissing and snuzzling. A most warming picture and one, perhaps, unexpected because of our own prejudices, reinforced by media depictions of sexless and priggish Chinese characters.

My first impressions of Aric are all confirmed. He is a wonderfully funny, mean, gentle, brilliant person. I told him that intuitively I knew that he would be the one true intellectual score for me on this trip, the person I would most like to know. He was genuinely embarrassed by the confession. Like me, he is critical of most of us here — in particular our sense of self-importance. But he is more understanding and forbearing than I, less willing to make critical snap-judgments about people on nothing more than the knee-jerk impressions that too often govern my life. On the other hand, once he does make critical judgments, he can be merciless in his biting wit — all excellent qualities for the Senior Editor of Newsweek magazine's Justice section.

We talked about everybody. He confirmed my suspicion that Dinni's and Bill Josephson's friendship predates this trip considerably, which is why he exerts such intense influence over her decisions for the group. Aric has also known Bill for a long time, Aric's wife having worked at the same law firm.

I told him how disgusted I have grown with the "whites only" policy and of my resolve never to enter another Friendship Store. But, as Aric pointed out, I'm being rather selective to single out the Friendship Store to boycott. What about our hotels? And the evenings' entertainments? And the restaurants? And the special currency? Etc. etc. As a native Californian, I'm familiar with the Chinese Exclusionary Acts. I just wasn't prepared to find them operating in China. I wonder if the best policy is "when in China, do as the..." er, well, Americans do.

We walked past some wonderful scenes tonight (in addition to the smooching ones I already described). Three young men stood outside the window of one house peering in over the heads of the family inside gathered around the TV. We walked by a theater of some kind, which was very popular judging from the numbers of people standing around and entering and exiting. All of them were Chinese.

But the best part was finding a playground that, even at that late hour, was being used by dozens of teenagers. My favorite "game" was a large metal wheel on a stationary platform— really two wheels joined by an axle, like a huge metal spool. Boys took turns standing between the wheels, planting their feet at one end and grabbing hold of grips at the other so that their arms and legs became spokes of the wheel, and then rotating faster and faster, like a pinwheel on the Fourth of July. Aric and I got dizzy watching them. They invited us to try it, but, chickens that we are, we both declined. It was another one of those frustrating moments when I cursed myself for having spent three years living among the Chinese without having learned Mandarin. ("Don't study Hakka," my students used to scold. "That's a common language. Learn Mandarin. It's for educated people like you." But I was interested in learning the language of their parents, which, in almost all cases, was exclusively Hakka, substantially different from Mandarin.)

Teenagers playing in a public park at night become living spokes

When we got back to the opera, it was still going on. We waited in the lobby for a few minutes, seeing the last ten minutes of the action through the open doors. When the group came out with the rest of the crowd, which was majority Chinese for a change, they were a little numb. After more than two hours, the opera was only half over. This was intermission!

Nobody wanted to stay for the second half, so we boarded our home-away from-home-away-from-home, and returned to our lakeside manor.

More tomorrow.

June 5, Wuxi Pre-School

As we made our way to the spacious and gracious Chiching Garden this morning after breakfast, the "real world" intruded into our fantasy — a not-so gentle reminder of what we left behind and what we will soon return to. Our local Wuxi guide, Mr. Liu is a funny and gregarious soul whose enthusiasm for his hometown is infectious. He had stayed up late into the night translating news headlines into English, which he read to us, painstakingly, on the bus ride into town: The President of Bangladesh was assassinated six days earlier, a time lag which served as dramatic illustration of our isolation here, an isolation that most of us on this tour savor.

Mr. Liu laboriously continued to bring the world into ours: Israeli gunboats peppered a guerilla base in Lebanon with mortar fire; the Pope left the hospital to return to the Vatican. Like an addict, I craned my neck from the back of the bus in order not to miss a single morsel of news, to be caught up, to be current, to know what is going on. And when it was all read, I was grateful to be here, in the not-quite-real world, where it is easy to exercise my willing suspension of disbelief.

The garden is the most beautiful we have seen so far. The lily-padded ponds are surrounded by white-walled corridors with graceful Chinese roofs of brown tile and an intricately-carved wooden railing. Along one of these corridors is a small pavilion built by some local chess-freak potentate centuries ago as a permanent setting for his beloved chess marathons.

My favorite structure in the garden was a small pagoda with a wall in back with a large window, and two pillars in front. What I liked most about it was its roof, a perfectly square tiled roof whose four corners came to upswept peaks, like the frosting on a chocolate cake. If you looked at it head-on from any side, the curved line of the roof looked like the smile of Alice's Cheshire Cat. Adding to this wonderland effect, an old man doing his tai chi exercises next to the pagoda was so beautiful in his controlled movement, that we watched transfixed for fifteen minutes or more. The old man, this perpetual slow-motion machine, seemed totally oblivious to our presence.

That visit helped dispel the reminder of death and destruction that came with breakfast. But it wasn't until the bus pulled up in front of the Qiaoyi Kindergarten that I was again thoroughly ready to give myself over to the unreality of being here, in the long-forbidden Middle Kingdom.

Scores of white-smocked children stood in the gateway to the school applauding our arrival and chanting their welcome in Chinese. From the balconies of the two-storied building, scores more waved at us with paper flowers. Many others continued playing in the courtyard outside. They played a combination of tag and blind-man's buff, with some children wearing huge papier-mâché heads that gave them the look of hilarious midget monsters in pursuit of the unadorned child who tried to stay out of arms' reach (but who loved getting caught so that roles could be reversed). The children shared their games, with only the slightest hesitancy in breaking away so that the next kid in line could take her or his turn. On a chair in the corner, in the shade provided by the overhanging eaves, sat a large white porcelain vat containing cold water.

Kindergarteners playing Chinese version of blind man's buff

We went from class to class watching the children at various activities. They sang wonderful songs for us, pantomiming various roles as they sang. They danced. They recited.

The difference between Chinese and Japanese children — at least in relation to foreign strangers — is dramatic. The sometimes excruciatingly painful shyness of Japanese children, and often of their adult families, was nowhere in sight here.

The kids were charmingly outgoing and seemed completely at ease with the intrusion of 31 Americans trooping in and out of their classrooms in different-sized clumps.

I stuck my head into one apparently empty room, only to find a woman wearing a white cap and white apron with a large red star on it, ladling out soup into small bowls. The delicious aroma in the room suggested there was more than just soup for lunch. Unfortunately, their lunch was our cue to leave.

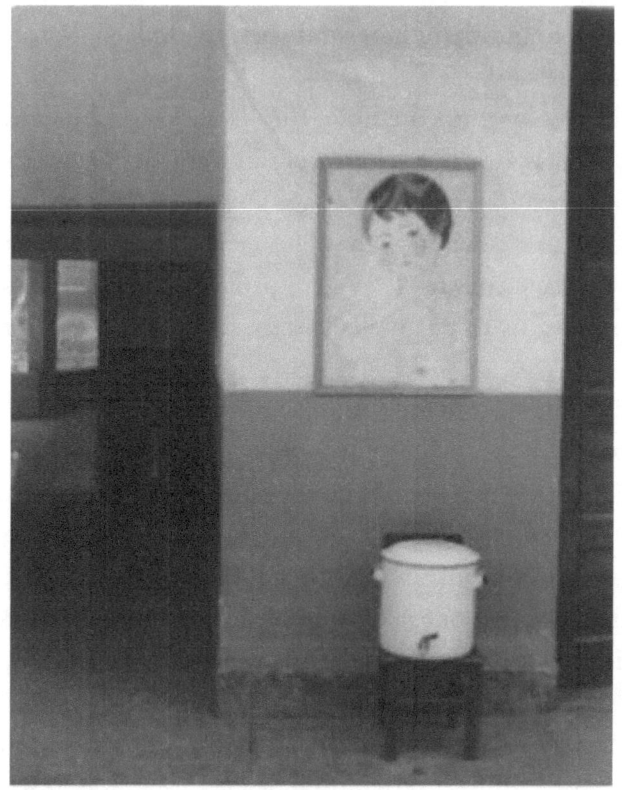

Fresh water cooler in kindergarten yard

As we did, the children again swarmed around us, pressing their hands into ours, clapping, sending us off as warmly as they had greeted us.

Aric, homesick for his own two baby daughters, the older in kindergarten, resisted the temptation to hold these children up as models, examples of what we might be able to achieve at home, if only we had the political will. Instead, he argued that these kids are probably no more impressive than a class of our own creative pre-schoolers. And I trust that he's right, though that doesn't mean that we can't learn something about childhood education from what is happening in China.

Four and five-year-olds at play are irresistible wherever you find them. But we found them here, and they are, indeed, both impressive and irresistible.

On our way back to the hotel for — oh joy — our own lunch, I asked Mr. Wong why the teachers were all women. He said that women were more suited to teaching that age group. He knew of not a single man who was an elementary school teacher! (Surely, there must be one or two in this vast country.) "Well," I probed, "what if your son, when he grows up, wants to be an elementary school teacher? What would you say?"

"I'd tell him," he told me without a moment's hesitation, "that that's women's work."

After lunch (which should be the title of an American travelogue of China), we went on a cruise of Tai Hu Lake, which, we were told, is among the most beautiful in China. I didn't find it all that beautiful (my maxim, "Been on one lake, been on 'em all," seemed appropriate to the occasion), but it was a wonderful excursion, like a family picnic in the middle of an endless summer.

On the way to the lake, we stopped at a silk farm where we saw an example of Chinese agricultural science that was fascinating. In a systematic and planned way, the Chinese build whole ecological systems: they raise sheep, not just for their wool and meat, but for their manure, which fertilizes the mulberry trees; these trees produce the leaves, which not only feed the silkworms, but are used as fodder for the sheep during winter. The silkworm droppings are used to feed fish that live in the upper and middle levels of fish ponds under the mulberry trees. The droppings of these fish feed plankton, which serve as food for the mud-dwellers at the bottom of the pond. The silt — now enriched by the droppings of the fish at the bottom, which have been enriched by the droppings of the fish in the middle and top, which have been enriched by the droppings of the silkworms, which have been enriched by the mulberry leaves, which have been enriched by the sheep droppings

— is then used as fertilizer to spread on rice paddies.

The whole process reminded me of that old song about the foot bone connected to the ankle bone, connected to the shin bone, connected to the hip bone, "now hear the word of the Lord."

Our lake cruise took us to a small island where we walked around, played, posed for countless pictures, and just had a really good time.

Judge Lane, that lecherous but lovable Federal judge, got his wife to take a picture of the two of us. Sally, who is almost as tall as the judge, but only half as wide, affectionately tolerates being called Mommy by him. The judge put his arm around my shoulder, and then, just before telling Mommy to snap the picture, got me to smile broadly by whispering, "Do your underwear say Jobs Not Jails, too?" According to my traveling companions, I have a different color or design Jobs Not Jails T-shirt for every day of the week. (I brought enough to give as gifts, and gave three away to the young, live-in workers at the State Guest House in Beijing.)

Federal Judge Art Lane just after asking me if my underwear also say "Jobs Not Jails"

On the way back, I sat on the roof of the boat's cabin to get the most out of the sun, and listened to NCCD's David Mintz deep in conversation with Mr. Wong. Mr. Wong has taken a strong fancy to David, calling him, unselfconsciously and without sexual implication, "lovely young man." (Lovely Young Man himself is getting fed up with the teasing this title has sparked.) They were talking about the Revolution, the law, the Constitution and the future. David is brilliant, but there is something about him that turns me off. He has that touch of arrogance born of brilliance and beauty that always makes me feel he is being tolerant of those of us not fortunate enough to have his political savvy.

I confess that my view predates this trip. I met David at NMPC's (the Prison Moratorium's) Kansas conference last year, where he lectured us about "political reality" which, he insisted, dictates forming alliances with anyone who shares a particular objective, regardless of whatever else you may disagree about. Since opposition to new prison and jail construction is often based on race and class objections (we don't want "their kind" in our neighborhood), he was telling us to coalesce with Nazi skin heads or worse. In itself, that advice is not without merit. An argument can be made that if we want to be effective, we must multiply individual objections by creating temporary alliances. One of the most common criticisms I hear about my own organizing style is that I am too skeptical of even "well meaning" corrections officials and government officials "who have an honest disagreement with you about the death penalty."

But I have worked in such uncomfortable coalitions of the incompatible, so I know it's a tactic that must be considered, but one which strikes me as a rarified variation of the means-justifies-ends logic. But regardless of the merits of his advice, it was the condescending manner in which it was delivered that I found most objectionable.

There was a touch of the self-reverential "expert" — a three-piece suited organizer telling the assembled, seasoned organizers all, that we were politically naïve if we thought we had any chance of success if we refused to work with racists or misogynists or Nazis, just to keep ourselves pure. It was as if he was indulging well-meaning, but ignorant and impotent children.

Yet, if that presentation was an example of his effective organizing style, I'll stick to my childish principles. In a room filled with jeans-clad, T-shirted professionals, you do not want to come across as a slick, young, glib lawyer (which David isn't, by the way — a lawyer, that is, glib or otherwise). It's only fair to point out here that Kay, who is very fond of David, thinks that he and I are alike in many ways. Both of us, she points out, are best at one-man operations, and slightly impatient with everybody else. Whatever the similarities, they don't overcome the discomfort I feel around him.

Anyway, there was "Lovely young man" this morning discoursing on historical imperatives, delving into the Marxist dialectic, and generally revealing a knowledge the rest of us lack, while taking dozens of photographs with the most elaborate and expensive camera equipment of anyone on this trip. What is it about my upbringing that makes me believe dedicated radicals should forgo the pleasures of wide-angle and telephoto lenses, not to mention red and yellow filters? Probably related to my impoverished past. And present.

On the way back from the lake, the bus stopped briefly at a goose farm where eight or ten of us got out to take pictures. Dinni seemed especially taken with the hundreds of geese surrounding the little wooden house at the end of the dirt driveway. The driveway was like a tiny peninsula into the lake. Besides the geese, wooden boats which looked like entire families lived on them floated on the lake around the house. They had straw mat roofs, bamboo poles and baskets lying all about, and straw-hatted adults at various tasks, with bare-headed children running among them, squealing and laughing. I would have liked to stay more than the two minutes we did, but the group was anxious to return to the hotel — and dinner.

Wooden boats behind goose farm

Had I known what was for dinner, I, too, would have wanted to hurry home. We began with the most beautiful hors d'oevres — and I mean beautiful in the Japanese style of pleasing every sense, from the esthetic to the palate — of fish and vegetables in the shape of butterflies. The wings were pieces of dark slices of fish bordered by lighter shrimp and cucumber, and the body was yellow radish slices; two long, curving onion shoots served as antennae. Then came the main courses, generous samplings of the local cuisine: spareribs, fish and eel. The latter was deep-fried and crunchy, an extraordinarily delicious dish, which I ate about four helpings of — and still looked on in pain as the plate of eels from the table next to ours was cleared away before I had a chance to finish what they had only barely touched.

My appetite for Chinese food is so insatiable that Judge Lane, when he and I are sitting at the same table, like tonight, has a whole routine ready. He waits until everyone else has pushed away from the table slightly, the better to let their stomachs spread, then shoves the abundant leftovers in front of my rice bowl, telling me loudly enough for everyone to hear, to finish them off, as only I can. I'm not embarrassed to say that, generally, I oblige. In fact, I've been obliging that particular request so faithfully that, under my beard, I've begun to look like that photo of me in my baby album, under which my father has written, "Three months old and still fat as a pumpkin." All things are as they were then, except... I am here.

Pearl West, Director of the California Youth Authority, contemplates hors d'oerve in the shape of a butterfly.

We have only one official visit tomorrow — to the Middle School, which, as you might imagine, I'm looking forward to in a very personal way, having taught for three years in a Chinese Middle School. After that, we are boarding the magnificent train once again, this time bound for Suzhou. ("In Heaven there is Paradise," our guidebook quotes a Chinese proverb, "on earth, Suzhou.")

•••••••••••••••••••••••••••••••••••

There is something first-class in the Old World sense about Chinese trains — more suited to Czarist Russia than a modern People's Republic. The small table with ashtray and flower vase that sits between the plush, upholstered sofas that face each other serves as my writing desk. My head occasionally lolls against the antimacassar...

•••••••••••••••••••••••••••••••••••

High School, A High Point

Leaving Wuxi this morning was not easy for me. If I ever come back to this country — and I would very much like to — that is where I would like to spend much more time. This morning's visit to the Chinese Middle School was, predictably for me, the high point — so far — of a trip characterized by its peaks.

The students and teachers who greeted us with the requisite applause were obviously very proud of their large, brick school in a beautiful setting of trees, vegetable and flower gardens, and a small animal farm for teaching animal husbandry.

I was immediately befriended by a man named Wu whom I took to be a senior student at first. He didn't look more than 18 or 19. But he is actually 31, and he teaches English here. While the rest of the group followed the school guide around the campus, listening to his explanation of this exhibit or that, I got a personalized tour by Mr. Wu who almost never left my side. I told him that I had taught English to Chinese high school students in Malaysia, and that I would very much like the opportunity to teach an English class here. He loved the suggestion, and hurried off to the principal to see if it could be arranged.

As we walked into the main building there were signs in Chinese, which we were told exhorted both the student body and the teachers to serve the people. The teachers' slogans urge them to value manual labor. The students' slogans extol the virtues of authority.

We went into a math class where most of our group stood at the front of the class, behind the teacher, watching and being watched. A couple of us made our way to the back of the class where we found empty chairs next to students we could observe. A student scooted over to make room for me to sit at his desk, which I did.

In the middle of the lesson, there suddenly came a clear imperative of some kind over the PA system in the classroom, and students immediately closed their books and put their fists carefully to their eyes, then laid their hands flat on the desk in front of them. Clearly, they were being led in eye exercises. Though I couldn't understand any of the commands, it was easy to figure out what was being said by watching the students respond with different types of exercises. Plus, I could understand the rhythmic count in Chinese (*"Yi, er, san, suh, woo, liu, chee, ba…"* — one, two, three, four, five, six, seven, eight) spoken quickly and deliberately like numbered steps in a rumba. Later on, we saw the entire student body do their daily exercises out on the field, also in counts of eight.

After the math class, we trooped into an English class taught by the senior English teacher, an old man in a blue Mao suit whose flattop haircut gave him the look of a stern disciplinarian, but whose obvious devotion to his students turned him into a Chinese Mr. Chips in my eyes.

"Do you always eat noodles for breakfast," his powerful voice boomed, stretching out "always" to cue his students. "No," came the assertive reply from a small student near the back, "I sometimes eat pancakes for breakfast." A perfect English pattern! I wondered, in fact, if this was a kind of "demonstration lesson" — the sort of thing that Mrs. Wong, the senior English teacher in the Chinese high school where I taught, always had ready to perform on a moment's notice, should anyone from the Education Department pay her an unexpected visit. But listening to more questions and answers convinced me that this was an ordinary class of extraordinary ability. Mistakes were made and corrected in that powerful voice, which never conveyed anything but affection.

Another command issued from the loudspeaker on the wall, and students rose immediately and moved out of the classroom. We followed them out to the playing field, where all the students were lining up to do their morning exercises.

There were hundreds and hundreds of students now standing in long lines — perhaps 50 rows of them — facing an outdoor stage on which one beautifully-braided teenage girl stood (along with all 31 of us) as a role model for the others to follow. Incredibly, the entire student body had left their classrooms, walked briskly out to the field, and arranged themselves in disciplined lines in a matter of five minutes. I leaned over and whispered to Mr. Wu that it would have taken twice that long in an American high school just to get the students out into the hallways, much less lined up on the field and ready.

As I surveyed those beautiful students, one of the things that struck me was how colorful they looked. Although some of them wore the blue or gray Mao suits that looked like uniforms, most wore bright pink and blue and yellow and white tops, though virtually all wore dark trousers. It was an improvement over the all white uniforms that my students had to wear. The diversity of color makes me think that the farther south one travels from Beijing, or, perhaps, the farther one travels in any direction from Beijing, the less rigid and more colorful the people become.

Students line up quickly to do series of exercises, led by a fellow
student

Again, we watched students perform exercises to loud-speaker
commands in counts of eight. They stuck their right legs and arms out
together, then their left. They did deep-knee bends, rotated their arms,
assumed martial arts poses, and obviously enjoyed it all. To our surprise,
the bus driver, our local guide, Mr. Wu, and Mr. Wong all joined a line
at the edge of the field and took part in the same exercises, "because it's
good for you," Mr. Wong explained later.

After this, the students went back to class and we went to the
standard question and answer period with the principal, who, Mr. Wu
had come back to tell me sadly, refused to let me teach a class. Mr. Wu
thought he was too nervous at the thought of a "professional English
teacher" and native speaker exposing the weakness of his local teachers.

In the middle of the debriefing session ("Our school ranks first
among the 90 middle schools in this province..."), Mr. Chips came

in with his English language students because, as he explained with the same bombast he used in teaching, this is "a once-in-a-lifetime opportunity for my class to hear real English spoken."

I was thrilled, of course. But my thrill slowly gave way to dismay and finally to anger as first one, then another member of our group took this opportunity, of all times, to make political speeches that none had made at previous sessions — not in front of the law school faculties, not in front of the Ministers of Justice, and not in front of the prison warden.

This series of high-minded talks, in vocabulary and subject matter that made no accommodation to foreign language students, may have been set in motion when dear Karamoko got up, in answer to a student's question about Abraham Lincoln, and explained why he thought America's celebration of Lincoln's birthday was hypocritical, an invention of American white people to expiate guilt. This prompted Bill Josephson to extol the virtues of Chinese Communist education as compared to American public education, which "doesn't teach." He elaborated at length on the differences between the two systems, boring even us who could understand him. Then, someone else got up to protest the characterization of American education as inferior, and someone else — Pebble — rose to defend our private schools as offering the only really decent education for the young. And on and on.

As I watched the faces of the students grow more and more confused as they understood less and less of what they heard — confirming the principal's fear of their inferiority — I grew more and more appalled. It was clear that not even Mr. Chips could follow the exchange of increasingly heated accusations and denials and declarations of principle regarding the efficacy of the American educational system, not to mention frequent and passionate flights into American history and political philosophy.

Now, I am probably the most outspokenly political person in this group. But to pick this occasion, to use this setting, to stake your political stand here just seemed exploitive to me. My traveling companions, high muckamucks all, had a captive audience, and they made the most of it.

In growing dismay, born of teaching experience, I passed a note to Dinni (who had a troubled look on her face, suggesting that she shared some of my discomfort, if not some of my disgust) asking her to introduce me as an English teacher who wanted to share a few words to this English class. She couldn't do this for some time, while various members of the group had their say, but finally she did introduce me as someone "who taught English to Chinese students."

I didn't know exactly what I would say, but I opened my mouth and the words just came out. I said that I had not only taught Chinese students for three years, but had taught English for a total of ten years, and knew good English language students when I heard them. I congratulated them on being able to speak good English, and congratulated Mr. Chips — who was beaming — for having taught them well. I told them that mastering any new language requires making fools of ourselves, from time to time, so they ought not to worry about that.

"There is a trick to learning a new language," I said, "and you have clearly learned that trick. It is to speak, speak, and speak again." Finally, I reminded them of the slogan I had seen in Mr. Chip's classroom: "A foreign language is a weapon in the struggle of life!" I instructed them, with appropriate gestures, to look around.

I paused, while they looked around, and then continued. "We are a group of Americans who are the best educated class of people in our country. We are lawyers and writers and judges and government officials. Yet, none of us can speak a word of Chinese. We are functionally illiterate, despite our riches. Your ability to speak English is a weapon that needs constantly to be sharpened. But the weapon is already in your hands, and that is your great achievement. All of you have earned our respect and admiration. I congratulate you."

Mr. Chips led the students in applause. I felt like a hero of the People's Republic, and a familiar sense of warmth engulfed me. There was communication between me and "my students" here, in this room. I wanted to freeze the moment. If I had been offered a job teaching at that school, at that moment, I wouldn't have hesitated for a second before accepting — but there are no foreign high school teachers in China, yet.

Later, on the bus to the train station, Mr. Wong sat by me and told me that my speech had had a powerful effect on the students and teachers alike, and criticized me for being so brief. I told him I didn't think my colleagues shared his assessment, and he said, "Yes, I knew that is why you didn't speak longer. But the students wanted to hear more."

Before we left the school, Mr. Wu and Mr. Chips both shook my hand and thanked me, and the students surrounded all of us as we made our way back to the bus.

Now, we are about to arrive in Suzhou, but my thoughts are still in that high school in Wuxi. And they will be for a very long time.

Our wonderful guide, Mr. Wong, and me

June 6, Suzhou Arrival

This may prove an interesting stop for reasons entirely unanticipated. Judging from what occurred this evening, I think an incipient rebellion is brewing.

After the short train ride from Wuxi, we were met by our local guide, another Mr. Wu, who is the most officious and correct-looking of all our guides, to date. Before being taken to the hotel to check in and "freshen up," we visited yet another garden (which was quite beautiful), and the itinerary for this stop was read to us: two more gardens, a sandalwood fan factory, an embroidery factory, and a local singing and dancing talent show for the benefit of "our foreign guests."

It may have been the absence of any substance in our planned activities that sowed the seeds of rebellion. (My colleagues seem endlessly concerned that there be enough professional activity to justify a tax deduction for the expenses they've incurred on this trip, though I do not make enough or own enough to itemize any deductions.) I think, though, that it's more likely a combination of our exhaustion and the temperament of our local guide that made tonight's flare-up inevitable.

We're all suffering from the "if-it's-Tuesday-it must-be-Suzhou" syndrome. But I'm getting ahead of myself.

First, Suzhou is a very beautiful city of canals and sycamores, like Nanjing, but much smaller. It is at least 3,000 years old, and famous for its silk and its gardens. This morning's garden visit was one of the most pleasant we have had — except that Mr. Wu's associate, Miss Lu, had a particularly obnoxious way of keeping the group intact and close: she used a bull horn! On the other hand, she was easy enough to ignore by falling farther and farther behind, as most of us did.

Suzhou canal

The large garden, with its trees and ponds and pagodas, was built about five hundred years ago by a corrupt politician who used his position to extort a fortune, according to the official patter. With that fortune, he built this garden, named — with tongue in cheek — "The Garden of the Humble Administrator."

The Garden of the Humble Administrator

I found myself in a small group which included Dinni, who spent her time expressing anguish over her crisis of conscience — what to get her husband for his birthday. "What do you get the man who has everything, who is a Marxist who doesn't value material possessions, and who has been to China," she wondered aloud. She was nonplussed by my suggestion — "Get him nothing, of course." Instead, she settled on a most exquisite Chinese scroll. I'm sure the Marxist who has everything will love it.

After the garden, we were taken to the hotel, which, unlike the others, is right in the middle of the old city. We had another glutton's supper and were supposed to meet at the bus by 7 p.m. for the talent show. For reasons that I can only attribute to very good sense, Kay and Aric and I decided not to go, but instead to stay at the hotel (no Chinese allowed) and shop. After browsing in the various shops off the hotel lobby, we decided to go for a walk. We were on our way out when, to our astonishment, one of our couples, Bob and Fran Smith, walked back in. The bus had only left less than half an hour before.

"What happened," we all asked at once. "We didn't expect to see you for hours."

"We walked back," Bob said through clenched teeth.

"Everybody should have," added Fran, out of breath and furious. "Why? What happened?"

The story they told has now been told and retold, over and over, by virtually everyone on the bus, with permutations and additions, but the same essential elements. When the time to board the bus, 7 o'clock, came and passed, there was, as usual, a group of stragglers. Mr. Wu, who believes strongly that punctuality is next to godliness (which is next to obedience) ordered the bus driver to leave without them. With Dinni and many others yelling to stop the bus (though just how forcefully Dinni ordered the bus to stop is one of the disputed elements of the story), Mr. Wu and the bus driver simply ignored them.

Among those not yet on board were Judge Art Lane and his wife Sally, as well as Maggie, the wife of Judge Bader-Mann — Judge B.M. That cantankerous old judge, stoop shouldered by the weight of his 70+ years, became the instant hero by standing and demanding to be let off the bus, which stopped, still within view of the hotel. As all eyes riveted on him loping painfully back to the hotel to retrieve his wife (a sight I regret missing), the bus took off again. This was too much for Jim Galvin, who screamed, "Stop this bus!" Which the driver did, having traveled only about ten feet beyond where it had stopped to let the judge out. Jim got off and returned to the hotel (though we didn't see him until much later).

In retelling this story, many people expressed guilt that they hadn't joined Jim in his protest right then. Bob and Fran, for example, took too long to think about whether to join him or not, and were forced to walk all the way back to the hotel from the theater, a distance of a mile or so. They knew they couldn't remain with Mr. Wu and keep a civil tongue (though, apparently, everybody else managed to do just that).

In the meantime, Judge B.M., who had taken the elevator up at the same time his wife and the Lanes were on their way down, was finally reunited with them, and they all boarded the bus, which hadn't moved since Galvin's escape.

Although not everybody agrees on who did and said what when, they do all agree that Mr. Wu is a "son-of-a-bitch fascist" who is out to teach his spoiled American guests a lesson. Well, not quite everybody... Lynn Zeller agrees with Mr. Wu that, in fact, we are a bunch of spoiled Americans who refuse to follow simple directions, and don't care if we are late or not.

While both observations seem accurate to me, the perverse in me is eager to see how it all plays out tomorrow. My guess is that if Wu tries anything that remotely resembles dictating, if he acts in any way that even smacks of superiority, there will be a general uprising. And that could be fun...

Back to basics. While my roommate has recovered from his indisposition (something he ate, no doubt), I'm feeling pretty lousy myself. I think because Doug wanted the air conditioner on last night, and because my bed is right next to it, I have a terrible sore throat today. A couple of people — most often Lynn — have spent a lot of time unable to accompany us on various jaunts because of being under the weather. In order to keep me down, however, I'd have to be terminally ill, and the terminal would have to be in sight.

One final note on "the incident," as people are delicately referring to it. What passed for this evening's local entertainment — "for the enjoyment of foreign visitors" only — was, in the words of Polaroid

Bob, "a Chinese Ted Mack's Amateur Hour." The high mark of the show, apparently, was a Chinese man, heavily made up with lipstick and rouge, singing "O Solo Mio." I may slash my wrists for missing it!

June 7, A Morning Walk in Suzhou

I got up early this morning and took a long walk through the irregular dirt roads and pathways that meander through the residential areas, finally emerging into the open fields of rice and wheat that seem to stretch endlessly beyond the outskirts of this small city.

On the way, two gorgeous little boys, maybe 8 years old, followed me down the streets, across bridges, through narrow passages between houses, until, finally, I took their picture. They were disgusted with my camera for not producing a print on the spot, and walked away.

I passed a farmer ferrying his geese to market by boat. He stood at the back of the long, low wooden boat, poling it along the canal as his dozens of geese honked furiously from their below-deck hold. Half a dozen wooden buckets with curved bamboo handles were stacked around the man's feet. (Later, on my way back, I saw the same man standing on the boat's prow, selling the geese that now clustered in the water around him, honking contentedly.)

Farmer taking his geese to market

As I passed over a bridge leading out of the central part of the city, I watched the early morning market scene. People were squatting along both sides of the bridge selling an impressive array of colorful vegetables, poultry, eggs and meat. It was a familiar scene. It is from markets like this that I did my morning grocery shopping in Borneo.

My favorite hawker — and, judging from the size of the crowd that surrounded him, many people's favorite — was a man wearing the long, white apron of a butcher. He was sitting on a wooden sawhorse, three wire baskets of hogs' heads before him. One of the baskets was still full to overflowing, and I could almost make out the bemused smile on Miss Piggy's face, as she contemplated the fate of her bodiless head.

At street market, butcher with baskets of hog heads

As I walked slowly from vendor to vendor, two joggers — western tourists — passed without taking any notice whatsoever. The Chinese seemed to take no notice of them, either. And not much notice of me, for that matter.

I kept walking, though the paths grew narrower and narrower. In the distance behind me, I could still see the commercial buildings and apartment houses, some five and six stories high. But here, where I was walking, here along the canals, the houses were low, single family units. Most were of brick or cement slab, and many had sunflowers in front and other brightly colored flowers I didn't recognize. I passed women hunched over pots of water cleaning chickens to cook, men brushing their teeth, and groups of high school students on their way to school, eyeing me curiously as we passed.

Morning in Suzhou

Commerce on a Suzhou canal

Finally, I stepped between two houses and found myself out in the open. Before me lay the plush, verdant paddies of rice and fields of young wheat pushing up.

Behind me lay the city, a few red smokestacks belching blackness into the sky.

I walked along the river that separates the city from the countryside, feeling the euphoric sense of liberation, temporary though I knew it was, from the regimentation of group expectations. Up and down the river, rattle-trap boats of every description could be seen, their occupants buying and selling an impressive variety of products and produce among themselves. Then, just ahead of me, I saw a small boat, held stationary in the water by a long plank, one end of which lay on the boat's flat bow and the other on the shore. Toward the back of the boat was a small enclosure half as tall as a person, and behind it was a makeshift, precarious looking bamboo structure, whose thatched roof provided the only shade. Although the boat already seemed dangerously low in the water to me, three or four men repeatedly walked the plank carrying very heavy loads of earth onto the boat in large baskets, which swung from ropes suspended at both ends of a bamboo yoke that fit over their shoulders. (In every city we've visited, we've seen men and women hitched up like mules to long wagons, pulling huge loads of wood or cement slabs.) Two other men on shore kept filling the baskets with red earth from a gigantic pile they were working on. On the boat, the pile of earth in front of the cage-like bamboo enclosure grew higher and higher. Off to one side of it was a large wicker basket. At the very front of the boat, just to the side of where the plank touched, was a very large, wooden wheel barrow with oversize bicycle tires.

Boat loaded with building materials

Worker carries heavy loads of earth onto boat

As I stood and watched, the men caught sight of me, and, after a few more loads, abandoned their work to come over. Although they could understand none of my few words of Hakka (the Chinese dialect I had tried to learn in Malaysia), and none of them spoke a word of English, they crowded around me, asking in gestures if they could look at my wristwatch, touch my hair, try on my dark glasses, examine the Chinese coin around my neck.

While looking through my Jobs Not Jails bag, they spied my camera, and gesticulated wildly for me to take their picture. They wanted me to set some gadget on the camera so that I could be in the picture, too, but my camera, designed for the simple-minded (thank god), is not so equipped. So, one by one, they took turns taking my picture with the others. Then they waited, more and more impatiently, for the camera to disgorge its photos, ala Mr. Polaroid. They poked at the camera, questioned me, waited and looked, and finally got bored and drifted back to their back-breaking work.

It was almost time for breakfast, by this time, so I turned back. As I recrossed the bridge into town, a boat passed slowly underneath. It was identical to the one I'd just left, except that where the thatched shade contraption had stood at the back of their boat, a small white sail flapped uselessly in the calm morning air. Instead of earth, this boat was loaded to the gills with red bricks, piled neatly in three-tiered stacks.

Brick laden boat moves slowly on Suzhou canal

On the walk, I made another of my "profound" observations: when people here speak about us *wai guo run* (foreigners), they lower their voices politely, as if we could understand the strange sounds that we describe as sing-song. That struck me as another of those differences between the Chinese and the Japanese that make me so much more comfortable with the former. I remember how, in Japan, people talked aloud about us, as if we were not even in the room. (Once, in Kobe, I thoroughly embarrassed two giggling young women in an elevator discussing the size of my big feet — huge, by Japanese standards. Waiting until the elevator door opened where I wanted to get out, I turned and asked them — in Japanese — if they knew where I could buy shoes.) The Japanese simply don't seem to believe that anyone can learn their language, or eat their food, or master the use of "their" chopsticks ("*Jozu-desu, nei*!" Oh, how clever you are! You can use Japanese chopsticks!") Therefore, they see no need to lower their voices when speaking about us.

The Chinese, on the other hand, as residents of the Middle Kingdom, can't understand why everyone isn't speaking Chinese, or eating Chinese food as a matter of first choice, or using chopsticks. Since all sensible people would want to do what the Chinese do, it is best to lower your voice when speaking about others, lest they overhear you and are shamed.

So much for profound observations.

By the time I returned to the hotel, just in time to eat, I was invigorated and raring to go. Which we did, to the silk and sandalwood fan factory — an artist's treat. For a while, I loved watching the rows of artists, both men and women, painstakingly painting the intricate pictures of fish and birds and flowers that adorn the fans. But I soon got bored, as I would if I worked there (or in any factory, for that matter). I found myself wishing to be outside, even shopping along the narrow, tree-lined streets that are often wall-to-wall people. That seemed to be the general sentiment of the group, too, because after a brief discussion, plans to visit another garden this afternoon were scrapped in favor of free time for all. Without objection, the fascist Wu acceded to all our selfish requests, spoiling any chance for a general uprising — a disgusting display of good manners!

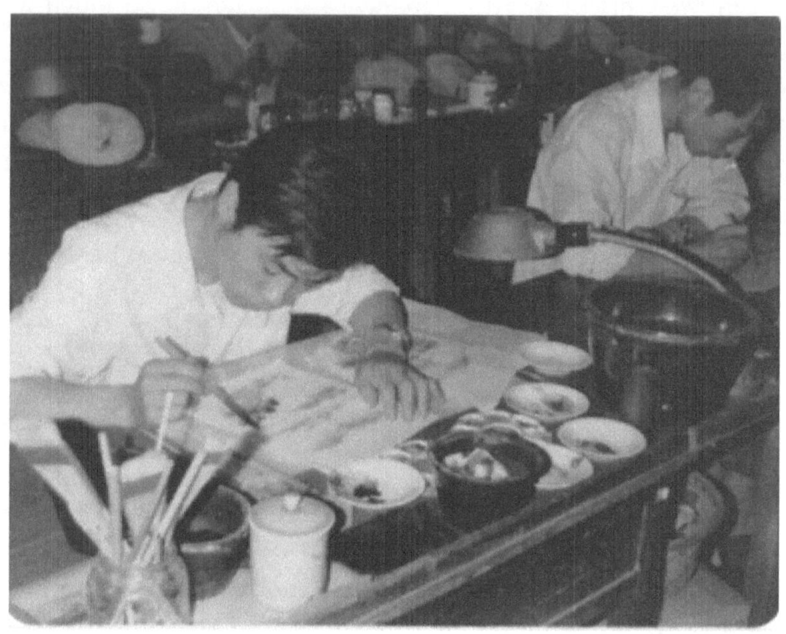

Silk screening at sandalwood factory

The bus deposited us in front of an antique store, many of whose treasures soon became the property of the propertied class. Pearl West, Bill Josephson, Ellen Schall and Steve Kelban spent the most, but nearly everybody, including Kay and Aric, dropped a bundle in that little establishment, proving yet again how well do-gooders do by doing good.

There was nothing in the store that I could afford, so I quickly left to walk around. Next to the antique shop was a narrow road, and on this road I found what I had not-so-secretly been looking for since arriving in China: a snake-oil medicine man. I couldn't tell what kind of snake the smiling huckster was holding, though it might well have been a cobra. But at his feet, in a see-through bag, there was another snake, a beautiful and completely harmless Chinese rat snake — at least

I think that's what it was — which I wanted. He made it very clear that it was not for sale. I think he feared that if I walked away with his "deadly" snake wrapped around my neck, his customers might begin to doubt the efficacy of his medicine. Or, maybe he just loved his snake. I left, disappointed.

In a while, Kay and Aric and I met up and went into a large Chinese department store. We became the center of attention wherever we went, drawing huge crowds around us at every counter we approached. Aric and I bought identical pieces of silk — magnificent deep blue silk with great bunches of lighter blue, yellow, green and white blossoms embroidered on it. It's really too beautiful for anything but a wall hanging. Kay tried on Mao hats and bought small gifts. Then we split up, agreeing to meet back at the bus in an hour.

I walked back across the square in front of the antique shop, this time going up the little lane on the other side. I wandered around a hardware store, and bought a hard hat (made of bamboo) and about two dozen beautiful wooden chopsticks in their own carved wooden holder for 50 fen (less than half a dollar). The dirt path led between a row of tailors on both sides, sitting in front of their shops behind tiny sewing machines, in competition with each other. People were buying material from the hardware store or the department store and taking it across the lane to the tailors to have something made, on the spot.

....

Snake Smuggler

Then I walked up the path toward a clump of trees at the end, where I found, to my delight, another snake show. The man had one of those beautiful little snakes I had so recently coveted. Through sign language, we managed to do a bit of business. The long and the short of it is that I, incorrigible snake lover that I am, was able to buy the lovely little thing with tiger stripes on its face and yellow bordered dark-chocolate saddles all down its back. I'm not sure what kind it is yet, but it is totally inoffensive and, I'm sure, non-poisonous. (I'm much surer it is nonpoisonous than I was about the non-poisonous snake in Japan whose bite put me in the hospital for three weeks...)

So, with snake stuffed inside my tote bag, I walked back to the hardware store to see if I could get a cloth bag to carry it in. They had the cloth on display, but it was in a long bolt. I played charades with the three young women behind the counter to try to make them understand that I wanted a bag, but to no avail.

Then, a group of Chinese who had seen me purchase the snake came in and spoke excitedly to the shopkeepers. They stepped back from the counter slightly, appraising this crazy foreigner in their shop. Then, the light dawned in the eyes of the youngest of the three, and she grabbed the cloth, measuring off a piece with her hand, inquiring with her eyes if this was right. I nodded, and she cut. Then she took the loose piece, ran outside with it, and in less than two minutes, was back with a perfectly-sewn snake bag.

Although the total cost of my purchase was three yuan — two for the snake and one for the bag — my treasure is every bit as valuable to me as the 500-yuan scroll that Josephson bought, or the 300-yuan basket the Schall-Kelbans bought. (As my mother is fond of saying, "Rich or poor, it's nice to have money.")

When we got back to the bus, Kay said, "Well, I got the most unusual gift." She unfolded a piece of cloth to reveal a beautiful mandolin. I was bursting to tell her that, extraordinary as her gift was, it didn't hold a candle to the uniqueness of mine. But Kay's own words of the day before kept resounding in my ears. She had said, responding to my numerous snake references, "Michael, I don't like to tell you what to do, but I think if people thought you actually had a snake, this group would be ripped apart." Trusting Kay's judgment completely, I decided to honor her advice. I did not say a word.

So, nobody knows I have a new pet, including my roommate, Doug. In fact, I had to use the pretense of writing to wait for Doug to leave our room long enough for me to water the little fellow in the bathtub. He drank long and deep.

Tonight after dinner, a bunch of us were sitting in my room drinking, when the subject of clearing customs came up. We all shared the various trials and tribulations we've experienced going through customs in different countries, as first one, then another of my companions shuddered at the thought of trying to get expensive antiques through customs without paying expensive duties. Aric, thinking he was making a joke, said that I was the craziest of the lot by trying to get a snake through customs. That insane notion conjured up such bizarre mental pictures (and was so far-fetched) that we all laughed at Michael. Including Michael.

Of course, Michael will actually have that insane problem to deal with, but not today. All in good time, my pretty, all in good time.

Tomorrow, we leave for Shanghai — and isn't that an incredible statement!

June 8, Shanghai

"Suzhou girls are reputed to have clever hands and quick brains," explained our guide this morning, as he took us through the Suzhou Embroidery Research Institute. That is why all the embroiderers here are women.

It was another factory tour, fascinating at first, but I was anxious to get to the train that would carry me to Shanghai. We were somewhat late leaving the factory because Jon and Anne, our dress-alike couple, bought a piece of embroidery at the last minute that, at 900 yuan or so, holds the record for the most expensive purchase. So far. Kay and Aric and I, the gregarious threesome, continually make fun of everybody for the amount of money they are spending. Absolutely flabbergasting! Of course, the three of us have been spending money, too, even as we joke.

A short time ago, after a brief train ride, we arrived here in Shanghai. Even the name conjures visions. Shanghai! City of history. City of myth and mystery.

We've been here long enough to have had a most unbelievable lunch (though considering the ghost of past repasts, it should not be so unbelievable... it's just that I'm so easily smitten by food). We ate on the 14th floor of the Hengshan Guest House, a huge and gracious old hotel built as an apartment house in what was known as the foreign quarter in 1936. Our room, on the 12th floor, has its own balcony, a bathroom big enough to house a family of four, and a commanding view of the city below. In half an hour, we leave for a city-wide bus tour, which, except for an acrobatic show tomorrow evening (Shanghai acrobats are world famous), is the only non-professional activity here. In addition to the foregoing, we will also visit a school for "bad kids," the Shanghai Prison, and a People's Court in session. Mercifully, no law schools.

From the 12th floor of the Hengshan Guest House, Shanghai spreads
below

No one has any inclination that I am smuggling a snake on this journey,
though there are endless jokes about where I might put one if I were
to smuggle a snake... All this joking has focused some of my attention
on the U.S. Customs Service, which Kay and I will face in Honolulu.
I'm a little nervous about it, but figure the worst that can happen
is confiscation (and likely incarceration at the Honolulu Zoo — the
snake's, that is, not mine).

I'm still feeling rotten, into the second day of a congested chest,
runny nose, hacking cough— the works! I should remain here and rest
as a number of others have done, felled by colds, but I'm always afraid
I'll miss something. On the other hand, I could curl up in front of
the TV and watch the daily fare of chemistry, physics and language
lessons. On the same hand, I could curl up in front of the TV and listen
while my fellow Americans poke fun at the chemistry, physics and

language lessons, smugly superior. The mocking tone seems shallow. We laugh at these "boring" televised school lessons, which are prepared and delivered by a government with educational goals for its citizens in mind, as if American television were not also full of goal-driven lessons. Instead of teaching science, however, the goal is consumption! And it is a lesson well learned, if this well-heeled group of well-educated Americans is any example. I wonder what the Chinese would think about "ring around the collar" and "Winston tastes good like a cigarette should."

After dinner, the group will be going out to shop at another Friendship Store, supposedly the biggest in China. That is one I'll definitely miss.

••

The Bund

We all went downtown after dinner tonight, the afternoon tour having been remarkably unremarkable, except in one detail, which I'll get to in a minute.

Tonight, the group was interested in the carpet store and the Friendship Store. I was not, though I went into the carpet store for a few minutes because I was with Aric, who wanted to buy a carpet. But I soon left, and Doug and I walked briefly along the wide, very popular walkway next to the Huangpu River. The riverfront is called the Bund, and it was filled with couples and families and groups of Chinese out for an evening's stroll. Despite my earlier promises to the contrary, I accompanied Doug to the Friendship Store just down a wide street from the Bund. (So much for principle.) But I determined to return, alone, to the Bund.

Shanghai's Friendship Store is actually several stores inside a walled compound. When Doug and I walked in, Lynn, Steve and Ellen, the most conspicuous consumers of all, were already there. Suddenly, I felt closed in, claustrophobic and struggling to take deep breaths. I had to get out. I'm not sure what or why I needed to escape so suddenly and so desperately. It might have been the four walls after my recent experience of outdoor freedom; it might have been the Chinese exclusion act; it might have been the atmospheric pressure to buy, buy, buy. Or, it might have been because I was sick. Whatever it was, I walked out quickly, passing Aric and some of the others on their way from the carpet store, and promised to meet him back at the bus in an hour. I walked back to the Bund.

I stood at the railing for a while, feeling the calming effect of the outdoor night air, and the anonymity, watching a large boat and smaller ones anchored here and there. Crowds of laughing, garrulous Chinese walked up and down, passing by without paying me any particular attention other than an occasional glance and whispered comment.

As I gazed out over the river, a strikingly handsome young man approached and started a conversation — despite the fact that he spoke no English and I no Chinese (except for half a dozen words or phrases, almost all having to do with food).

Still, with little difficulty, he was able to communicate a number of things, including his belief that America is a country of guns and violence. I'm not sure, but I think at one point he asked me which I liked better, Shanghai or America (a variation of a question I grew used to hearing when I lived in Japan). While we were "talking," another young man came along and said, clearly, "Good evening." Soon, a crowd had gathered and the first young man, sadly intimidated by the English fluency of several people in the crowd, said good-bye with his eyes and faded away. I was sorry to see him go, but exhilarated by this chance to speak to people on the street, in an unstructured, unplanned, unprogrammed setting. Even here, in this distinctly cosmopolitan city of eleven million people, a conversation with an English-speaking foreigner drew quite a crowd.

About four of those now gathered around me spoke English to varying degrees. We spoke of my work, their country, crime in both of our countries, English (they were all college students studying English), the phenomenon of having certain stores and hotels off-limits to ordinary Chinese ("We Chinese are used to that..."), the beauty of the night and of their city and country. In no time at all, I had to get back to the bus, though I yearned to stay longer. I am counting on coming back tomorrow night — after the court session, after the juvenile reformatory, after the acrobats — to talk to more people.

When I got back to the bus, feeling sick and, if truth be told, slightly envious of David Mintz's two carpets, Pearl West's silk carpet, Steve and Ellen's beautiful basket (for which I would happily mug them), I also felt almost euphoric, certain that I had had the best evening of all. Later on, Kay told me that she had also walked along the Bund tonight with Len Troppin, and that they had had a similar experience. She told me of meeting one middle-aged man who spoke of the difficulties of living through "these years of turmoil and uncertainty." When Kay asked what he meant by "these years," he looked nervously over his shoulder as if afraid of being overheard, and told her that nothing is settled. Kay was as energized by this exchange as I was by mine, though neither of us had spent a fen, nor brought back a single possession to show for the evening.

•••••••••••••••••••••••••••••••••••••

The Children's Palace

Remember when I said that we had done one unforgettable thing this afternoon? Well, that thing, which came at the end of the city bus tour, was a visit to one of the eleven Children's Palaces in Shanghai, one for each of the ten districts, and one Regional Palace. And Palace, indeed, is what it was.

First of all, it looked like a palace. It is a huge, Victorian building with great bay windows and a many-gabled roof. At the very top, is a gigantic five-point star of gold (color, that is) in front of a flaming red torch that looks like the ACLU symbol. It is a palace of unbridled (well, somewhat bridled) rambunctious recreation, free for all the children in this city, ages 6-16, and every city has them. Besides recreation, the Children's Palace is also a center of practical and moral (which, in China, is also practical) instruction. Outside on the grounds surrounding the Palace was a veritable cornucopia of children's delights — a jungle-gym set that lets those who reach the top come flying down by holding onto a bar that slides back and forth on pulleys, an obstacle course designed to put the kids in mind of the grueling conditions their Founding Mothers and Fathers suffered on the Long March, slides, narrow bridges over ponds, bean bags, board games, electronic games that teach hand-eye coordination, and — best of all — no adults in sight. At each play site, older children supervise younger ones.

The Children's Palace in Shanghai

On the inside there were lessons of all kinds. We were treated to a concert of classical Chinese instruments in the hands of ten-year-olds. We watched a group of budding eight-year-old ballerinas going through their paces, and I fell in love with an elfin-faced, Keane-eyed prima donna in blue tights. We were sung to by a mixed chorus of adolescents, and entertained by a dramatic poetry recitation. We were struck dumb as two six-year-old girls dazzled us with their ping-pong virtuosity, taking on all comers, and slamming back even the quickest of serves any of us could deliver. None of us managed more than one or two successful returns, and none of us earned even a single point.

Young violinists perform at the Children's Palace

On another floor, we saw an art class mastering a bamboo still life. Pearl complained that the instruction was all too rigid, too pat, too structured, too "inside the lines" to really qualify as art — but I kept wishing someone had taught me how to draw when I was their age. Another group of youngsters put together model planes and cars, and still another struggled through a creative writing class.

It was simply wonderful. To me, it was the most enviable institution I have seen in China so far, and, despite the criticisms that I have heard from a few members of the group (along Pearl's lines), I found nothing that I did not admire there.

Why do we put so few public resources into our children's development?

What we saw today made it clear, beyond words, that what it takes to nourish children as a national treasure is the will to do so. We have no national policy at all concerning children, no commitment to their creative instruction or systematic nurturing, nothing more than empty slogans that proclaim them our most important natural resource. What we have, instead, is a state-by-state, district-by-district commitment to public schooling, guaranteeing that the children of the most affluent receive the most resources, while poor children, who suffer from the absence of so many resources, will continue suffering from poor schools as well. We seem more concerned with punishing wayward kids in county juvenile halls and state "youth offender" prisons than in providing the kinds of constructive educational and recreational resources, available to all, that are so much a part of the Children's Palace, and which represent a real investment in the future of these kids and the future of the country.

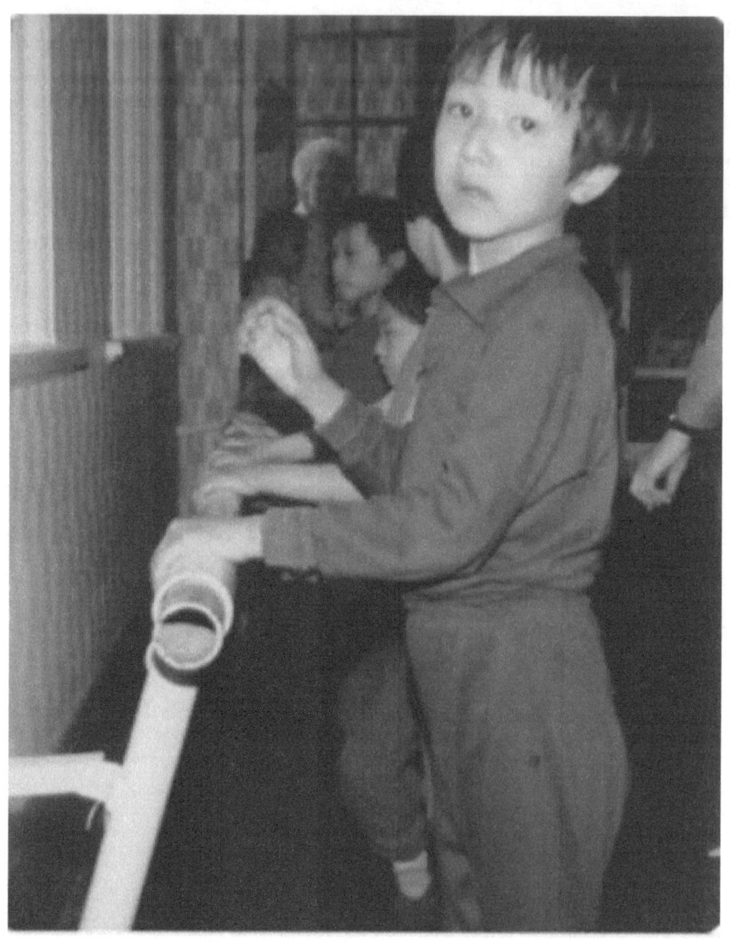

Young ballerinas at the bar, Children's Palace

I know Aric would object, accurately, that my indictment is too broad, too sweeping. He would point out that there are many good things about American education, and that we, too, have model centers for instructing children. Too often, though, those "models" are available only to those who can pay the price. The truth is, we have nothing comparable, to this thoroughly uplifting Children's Palace, this after-school center of learning and fun, and that is a sad commentary.

I will keep those very happy, very healthy children in my mind for a long, long time.

But I can't keep anything in mind at the moment. I can barely keep my stuffed head awake, so I'll end here.

June 9, Shanghai People's Court

I feel like shit, headachy, very congested, tired. But, by god, I will not be daunted. This morning — perhaps through the involvement of our friend from the Ministry of Justice — we are watching a proceeding in the People's Court, where I am writing this. This afternoon, we will visit the "special school" for delinquent juveniles. I have looked forward to that visit for days, so I wish I were more up for it. But I'm resolved not to collapse until it's all over.

This appellate court is fascinating, not least because of its physical similarity to American courtrooms. In the waiting room, there are long benches filled with people. Are they friends of the accused? Potential witnesses? Budding lawyers interested in the procedure? Just curious citizens? We don't know.

Inside, the courtroom is divided into three sections, separated by two narrow aisles, with benches for perhaps two hundred people. We are seated in the middle section. To our left, across the aisle, are Chinese spectators whose animated conversations contrast sharply with our respectful, even reverential hushed tones. Across the aisle to our right is another group of American tourists, this one a delegation from the American Bar Association.

(Incredibly, just a moment ago, Aric jumped up when he recognized his own father-in-law, a Harvard professor, among them. He had known his father-in-law was in China as a lecturer on international trade at the invitation of the Chinese government, and was hoping to rendezvous with him later on, in Hong Kong. But, he was dumbfounded to see him walk into the same courtroom in Shanghai just moments after we had walked in. And the world grows ever smaller.)

Behind a wooden railing — the bar — is a table, front and center, at which the accused sits with uniformed officers of the court. Behind the bar to our right is another table where the Public Procurator sits — a kind of district attorney who is charged with serving the interests of the People (as our DAs are charged with serving the interests of justice). To the left sit the defendant's lawyers. The judges' bench is raised, as in our courtrooms, and has three large chairs. Behind it on the wall is the great seal of China.

We all have earphones, and now a woman's voice translates into English the rules of proper courtroom decorum: no recordings, no video filming, no questions or speeches from the audience. We are allowed to take still photos, however, (and we are flashing away like crazy), as long as we stay behind the bar. No one seems at all concerned that I am sitting here scribbling away furiously.

She is now explaining the case that we will hear. It is an appeal of a nine-year prison sentence for bank theft. From her description, it is clear that guilt is not the issue here, but the length of the sentence. "The criminal" — the word she uses to describe the defendant, Wong Jau Ming — "used a bamboo and metal tool to steal 10,000 yuan ($8,000) from the bank where he was employed. While in custody for that crime, he confessed to an earlier act of larceny." There will be three judges to hear this appeal, and they will be "professional judges" because this is a trial "of the second instance" — an appeal. In an original trial — in the Primary People's Court — only one of three presiding judges is a professional, though the two lay judges have equal authority. I have no idea who selects these lay judges, or how they are selected.

It appears that the judges in this case "of the second instance" will be asked to decide between The Procurator, who thinks nine years is too lenient, and the defendant, who thinks it is too severe.

As the appellate judges come in (two men and a woman), both our group and the ABA group stand. The Chinese not only do not stand, but are laughing at us for doing so!

The Chief Judge asks the defendant many questions about his circumstances. He instructs the defendant that he can challenge any of the judges if he believes that they are already involved in his case. He can defend himself against any of the charges if he is not satisfied with his lawyers' defense. He will be given the opportunity to have the last word.

The Public Procurator, who speaks many times, maintains that the trial court erred in sentencing Wong to only nine years, since his crime is "a very grave one," and since it involves a violation of the public trust, inasmuch as Wong was employed by the bank he stole from. Then, of course, there is that matter of the other theft he confessed to — for which he was never indicted, much less tried or punished.

The defendant himself believes the sentence is too long because he confessed his crime, because he volunteered the information about the earlier crime, and because "I was in disorder, ideologically, at the time."

His defense lawyers, who rise each time the Procurator finishes, argue that the trial court did not make a mistake, that nine years is a fitting sentence, and that their client's cooperation should be weighed in the sentencing. The fact that the defendant and his defense counsel seem to disagree is startling, to say the least.

Back and forth the lawyers go, arguing for an increased sentence on one side, and for retaining the sentence on the other, refuting each point the other side makes exactly as they refuted it that last time they stood to make the same point. The judges ask many questions, and not merely of the lawyers. They conduct a lengthy interrogation of Mr. Wong himself. Although the presiding judge gives him a chance to have the last word, Wong has nothing to add.

Finally, after about an hour, the judges have retired to their chambers to render their decision — not in weeks or months, but now. We are told to wait for their return.

Now that the judges have left the courtroom, the Chinese part of the audience is again noisy, though few people — other than us Americans — move from their seats. The lawyers from our group have immediately mingled with the lawyers from the ABA group, and good-old-boy conversations are breaking out all around, amid the clicking of cameras and the flashing of bulbs. We have two local guides in Shanghai, the main guide, Ms. Liu, and her assistant, Mr. Xu, who tells us that he believes the court will impose a sentence of at least nine years.

After about fifteen minutes, the judges return. Again we stand. Again the Chinese chuckle, and remain seated.

The presiding judge stands and reads:

"The accused, Wong Jau Ming, committed the crime he is accused of. He also committed the earlier crime. The facts are proven, the evidence is conclusive, and the accused has confessed. This is a case of graft. The Primary People's Court was incorrect in thinking this was a case of theft. It is graft. The gravity of the offense is severe. The Primary People's Court did not render a sentence according to the gravity of the offense. The accused" (who stands with head bowed before the bench) "believes nine years is too much, but his reasons are unsound. The amount he stole was great, he was an employee, and he presented false evidence during the investigations. The case must be treated severely. The fact that the accused says he has turned over a new leaf must also be taken into account. Therefore, it is the decision of this court to revoke the sentence of the Primary People's Court, to impose a sentence of ten years for the crime of theft, to impose an additional sentence of one and a half years for the crime of graft, and to confiscate the wristwatch of the accused to make up the difference between what was stolen and what was recovered. This sentence is final, and cannot be appealed. Court is adjourned."

I have no doubt that the appellate decision had to have been reached before the "trial" began. It's too much of a stretch to believe that three judges could have retired to chambers, discussed the facts of the case and the applicable law, offered their individual observations, then sat and written a decision, all within fifteen minutes of having concluded the trial. It flies in the face of our notions of due process, and so undermines faith in the fairness of the process. On the other hand, the fact that Mr. Wong had to pay a higher price for having violated a public trust is refreshing, however one might disagree with the actual number of years meted out.

Wong Jau Ming, whose nine-year sentence had suddenly become an eleven-and-a half-year sentence, was led away, soon to be confined in the Shanghai Prison, which we will see tomorrow.

•••••••••••••••••••••••••••••••••••••

Reform School

We are about to go out for dinner, and then to an acrobatic show. I can't generate any enthusiasm for either. It is not the memory of defendant Wong being led away that has depressed me, but our afternoon visit to the Shanghai District Work and Study School — a juvenile reformatory under the jurisdiction of the Ministry of Education.

The school's stated mission is to "transform the students into useful persons for the Motherland." As you walk into the boys' facility (there are 200 boys, and another 50 girls in another facility just up the road), a large sign in both English and Chinese offers a "Warm Welcome." I'm not sure whom they are welcoming; there is electrified wire strung along the top of the wall.

The boys, who looked like any group of teenage boys, live in very sparse dormitories with 28 bunk beds in each. We visited a physics class in progress. Aric approached one of the kids in the second row, called our guide over, and began questioning the student. He was there for fighting, he said, and "hanging out in the streets." Later, during our debriefing, we were told that most of the students were there for fighting, petty theft, and "abnormal sexual relations" — a reference not to bestiality or sodomy, but to heterosexual premarital sex.

Then we saw the essence of what distinguishes this school from a regular school — the "work rooms." All students are required to work three hours a day to "learn discipline and skills." The skills that most of the boys were learning did not seem to have much practical application: one group was breaking down cardboard boxes, while another group assembled — or reassembled — the boxes that had been broken down so that they could be broken down again. Aric and I tried to question a couple of these boys, but they never stopped their work and never gave an answer that was anything less than fully devoted to their regimen. A school official stood next to us at all times taking notes.

We were hustled quickly out of the boys' school and back onto the bus for the short ride to the girls' school, where the briefing took place after our tour. We were told by the school officials that many of the children had bad home lives, and that "the ten-year Cultural Revolution spurred bullies, hooliganism and illiteracy."

Two things about that girls' school will always stand out in my mind. The first was a small warehouse-like room where ten girls stood around a table piled high with small boxes. We stood around the girls who stood around the table and, yes, we took pictures. Behind us lay thousands more small boxes, piled to the ceiling, awaiting repair. The girls worked quickly, picking up a box in front of them, putting a piece of adhesive tape on an outdated price left there from its previous use, and Scotch taping frayed edges. They spoke without visible emotion, as if giving rote answers to math questions. ("I love my new school... I never think of my former bad life, but only of my rewarding new one, as a contributing member of the Motherland.") They never stopped their work. When I asked what their most and least favorite things were about the school, none had a least favorite.

Then Aric asked one of the girls what she had done to be sent here. Like so many of the others, she was here for fighting and skipping school. The question itself infuriated Polaroid Bob, who said as we were walking out of the work-shed, "Never ask what they've done. No. Never. Always bad. Too personal. Not important..." to which Aric responded, "If you think that was bad manners, you should see me on a real interview."

Important or not, Aric's question elicited this additional response. "My father beat me. I would have been lost but for the new school. My teachers were patient and explained why my behavior was the wrong way. Now I've decided I want to be a useful contributor to my country."

Endless hours of mindless mending of paper boxes lay before them. But that is not the only "skill" the girls are taught in their three hours of forced labor a day.

We also visited a room with two dozen girls in it, each bent over a sewing machine. The boys, too, did more than endless breaking apart and reassembling cardboard boxes; they also assembled bicycles.

By the time we reached the briefing session, I was already thoroughly depressed. The principal turned away all questions that suggested that the school resembled a prison in any way. ("We see bars on the windows... We see electric wires on the fences...")

"Prisons are run by the Ministry of Public Security, which also operates juvenile detention facilities," he reminded us, "while we are under the Ministry of Education." Just how those facilities differ from this "school" he couldn't explain.

In the view of Principal Tiu, neither the bars, nor the electric wire, nor the three hours of forced but meaningless work a day, nor the ten-month regimen with once-a-week visits, qualified this place as anything other than a school. "After all," he concluded benignly, "these kids are not hardened criminals, but have only strayed from the correct path. After two months of voluntary confessions and eight months of labor, they can re-enter regular school, good as new."

Kay, as depressed as I, tried to determine how widespread the practice of detaining status offenders is here. Status offenses, like "hanging out on the street" and "fighting" are only "crimes" because of the status of the offender, in this case that of being a juvenile. (Those behaviors, if committed by adults, would not be crimes.) Kay asked half a dozen times how many students there are like these in China, but the only information she could get out of Principal Tiu was that Shanghai has eleven districts, and each has a school like this one. Aric also seemed overwhelmed by this visit, which is certain to find a place in whatever he writes for Newsweek.

How ironic that the euphoria I felt yesterday at the Children's Palace has evaporated in the face of these other children.

Even though I was able to discount the self-serving euphemisms ("We love our students back to the right way...") I was unprepared for the sad-eyed girls themselves, in their official presentation to us at our debriefing session with the principal.

Several told their stories, after considerable prodding from Principal Tiu in the same phrases we had heard the girls use in the box repair hut. But one girl lost her struggle to fight back tears, and had to give up her recitation. Then we were "treated" to "entertainment" — a heartbreaking experience that will be indelibly inscribed in my memory.

I was sitting just off to the side of the blackboard, where a line of girls stood facing us. They were dressed in bright colors, lots of reds and blues and whites, like the girls we saw yesterday at the Children's Palace. But yesterday's children were nowhere to be seen today. It was as if the enthusiastic performances we had seen at the Palace were being mocked by today's performance. As the girls sang — about going home — not one smiled. A few looked defiant, I thought, or hoped. I wondered how many times they had sung this song for their "foreign friends." The girl standing closest to me looked about 16 years old. As I watched her, I saw the tears welling up in her huge dark eyes, until they began to spill over. At first they came slowly, and then they poured down her face in steady streams. She did not wipe away her tears nor stop her singing. She made no move at all different from her solemn-faced companions.

It was an excruciating ending, and one which fit the occasion. At last the song was done and the girls, freed from their command performance, were allowed to return to their little paper boxes and their sewing machines.

······································

Shanghai Acrobat Troop

It is midnight. My sagging spirits, coupled with a worsening cold, did not dispose me well to any evening's activity. That probably also affected my review of tonight's dinner — good, but not outstanding. (Mercifully, I am not so sick that I can't eat.)

So, my reaction to our post-dinner entertainment was totally unexpected. We attended the Shanghai Acrobat Troop, which was nothing less than sensational. Magical. Marvelous. Not to mention boneless. They tumble and spill and roll and jump. They juggle and balance, do bird calls and funny little skits that are funny.

They roller skate on a tiny tabletop. They do serious dancing, with sinewy bodies of pure muscle and grace. They fly. And, best of all, their audience is primarily Chinese, who clearly love what they are seeing. Unlike so much of the entertainment arranged for the benefit of "our foreign visitors," acrobatic troops like these have been entertaining the Chinese since long before the foreigners arrived, and would continue to entertain even if there were not a single tourist left in China.

I will be singing their praises for many months, if for no other reason than that they have managed to bring me up from the depths to my old, smiling, cheerful self. The sadness I felt when I left the reform school this afternoon, I was certain, would not leave me for the duration of the trip. I'm embarrassed to admit that it already has.

June 10, A Shanghai Walk

I don't have much time to write before we set out this morning for the Shanghai Prison. But I want to describe my pre-breakfast walk, before the memory of it is drowned in the soul-squeezing emotion that I expect to wash over me during the prison visit, the same that washes over me during every prison visit everywhere.

I got up at six this morning, and set out to explore the tree-lined boulevards of the residential area where this Guest House is situated. Just outside, a large group of mostly senior citizens (with a few young people among them) were doing their morning Tai Chi exercises, and I watched, again, completely captivated by the intense concentration that must be required to be able to flow so effortlessly from near-pose to near-pose, never stopping long enough to capture a pose, a continuous, sinuous movement of graceful curves and lines.

Then, I walked on and discovered the morning market, half a dozen blocks of street vendors and shoppers — and one gawker, me. I stirred no extraordinary attention, although when I snapped a picture of a blind beggar, there was clear consternation in the voices of the people who watched me. He was old, perhaps 70, and he wore a blue Mao hat and suit, faded and patched. He used a long bamboo pole as a white-tipped cane, and carried a large tin cup as he walked, slightly bent, among the sellers on the sidewalk. He is the first beggar I have seen in China, unless you want to count the ragamuffins who hustled the tourists on the Great Wall.

Street market sellers were not happy with me for taking this photo of a blind beggar

The street market offered everything from chestnuts to fresh crabs, which an old woman cleaned, sitting on a small stool bent over a pot of water. There were people bartering onions for sugar beets, offering fried bread to hungry students on their way to school, and green vegetables of every description. Even at that hour of the morning, the streets were jammed with customers, mostly women in blue or gray pants and shirts, carrying simple baskets for their morning's haul. Occasionally, a bicyclist, usually a man, made his way uncertainly through the teeming streets. There were many women pushing many babies in bamboo strollers with roller skate wheels. (Are all Chinese babies beautiful?)

A smiling Shanghai mother pushing her baby in bamboo stroller

As usual, I returned to the hotel reluctantly. My morning walks — the only time I can have my very own thoughts about my very own experience — have made me love this country, or, at least, these people, as if there were ever any doubt.

After breakfast, we will visit the prison. The other night at the Bund, when I told one of the young guys I met that we would be visiting the prison, he said, "Oh, before the Revolution that was the largest prison in Asia."

"And now?" I asked.

"Now?" He thought barely a second before replying with a smile, "It is the largest prison in Asia."

After the prison visit, we are supposed to have a huge lunch (as if we've had any other kind) at the Park Hotel, a leftover from pre-WWII days when China was occupied by multiple nations and their armies — the French, the English, the Americans — all soon-to-be supplanted by the occupation forces of Imperial Japan. The Park Hotel is reputed to have the best food in Shanghai, if not the universe.

Before boarding the plane to Canton this evening, we have the afternoon to ourselves. On your mark, get set... travelers' cheques at the ready... Charge!

•••••••••••••••••••••••••••••••••

Shanghai in the 1930s

On our way to the Park Hotel for lunch, Ms. Liu told us that Israel has wiped out a nuclear reactor in Iraq, killing one or two people in the process. A lively discussion erupted around this incident, following fairly predictable pro-Israel anti Israel lines. I take a rather different view. As far as I am concerned, the destruction of a nuclear plant anywhere is a positive step. I am not naïve enough to believe it signals the dawn of a non-nuclear world, or that Israel, which guards its own nuclear stockpiles zealously, had such altruistic objectives in mind when its pilots strafed the plant. But, frankly, I don't care what their motives are. There is one less nuclear reactor in existence today than there was yesterday, and that is a good thing. (Actually, according to Ms. Liu, the attack occurred two days ago, proving again that the world can careen from crisis to crisis totally without my help.)

I wonder if I would feel the same way if Iraq had just bombed one of Israel's nuclear reactors. I hope so. I also have to confess a secret: admiration for the skill of those pilots. Their precision bombing wiped out an entire nuclear reactor and cost only one or two lives. (I grant you, "only" one or two lives is not that insignificant if you happen to be one of the one or two...) I feel guilty about that confession. There is something unseemly about someone who professes to be an antimilitarist praising the skill of a military venture. But still, there it is.

The Park Hotel lunch, though more abundant than even our enlarged large intestines have come to expect, was not the best food in the world. Not even in China. But it was a great gathering. First of all, from our 15th floor dining room, we could see the magnificent city of Shanghai stretching out below us. But second of all, and far more important, we were treated to a wonderful talk by Frank Bruder, an NCCD board member who lived here in Shanghai back in the 1930s as an employee of International Telephone & Telegraph, which set up the telephone system here before the war.

Frank is the oldest member of this tour, and, together with his wife Johnnie, the nicest. They are a truly charming couple. They love each other. Johnnie teases Frank about being "so much older" than she (ten years, maybe), but she obviously adores him. Not only do they treat each other in a way that warms you to watch, but they are unfailingly cheerful and kind to everyone else. Johnnie always gets a twinkle in her eye when she gently ribs Frank about his age. Somewhere in her late sixties, she is the warm and funny (not to mention bosomy) grandmotherly type.

Frank may be the oldest, but he doesn't come close to looking his near 80 years.

Judge B.M. looks much older. The twinkle in Frank's eye is every bit as bright as hers. They sort of remind me of Nick and Nora Charles, grown old together (though, in fact, they were married only a few years ago, after Frank's first wife died). I would venture to say that the Bruders are everyone's favorite couple on this trip.

Earlier, Kay and Aric and I had thought we would write an epic poem about everybody to be read at our final banquet. The idea fizzled (who has time to write poetry?) when our poems kept getting meaner and meaner. An exception are the ones we wrote about the Bruders. I wrote: "Frankie and Johnnie are lovers/He's been to China before/Johnnie's as warm as bed covers/And Frank's never ever a bore."

But it was Aric who captured them perfectly in this simple couplet: "There is no couple cuter/Than Frank and Johnnie Bruder."

Anyway, after lunch, no one cuter than Frank Bruder got up to tell us about the old days in Shanghai, when foreigners had their own designated part of the city, "the foreign quarter" — no unauthorized Chinese allowed — with their own personal rickshaw drivers, and servants to do their laundry, their cooking, their cleaning. They enjoyed a glittering night life that was cosmopolitan in the European sense — lots of French people fraternizing mostly with other French people, an abundance of English men and women chumming it up with other English men and women, and a motley collection of Americans mixing it up with everybody.

Everybody but the Chinese, that is. Nobody played with the Chinese but other Chinese.

Everyone's favorite couple, Frank and Johnnie Bruder with Kay Harris

It seems utterly incredible that less than fifty years ago, the French, English and American armies took turns marching down Shanghai's streets in dress-parade, the French on Tuesday, the English, Wednesday and the Americans, Thursday. It was just a "friendly display of force," a reminder to the Chinese, those uncivilized heathen, just who was in control.

Like most everybody else, I sat enthralled by Frank's story, which he told while Chinese waiters cleared our tables and Ms. Liu looked unhappy at the memory of those humiliating years. Frank was careful to make sure that everyone understood he was not longing for a return to those "glory days" — except in that wistful way we all long to return to our youth. He was explaining those days, and explaining how very few of the foreigners here ever thought about the nature of colonialism, or the implications of excluding the Chinese from their own country.

Apparently, however, not everybody understood Frank's story that way. At the end of his talk, New York City's Keeper of Women, the young, spoiled rich kid from Manhattan, jumped up to ask how Frank could possibly justify those days. "Didn't you ever think what you were doing was wrong? Didn't it ever occur to you that you were offending the Chinese then, and that you're offending them now?" Frank looked hurt, protested, then apologized if he'd offended anyone. That wasn't his intention, he explained. He only wanted to say how things had been then.

So, there we were, being told how to be sensitive to the Chinese people by a woman who had treated Mr. Wong like hired help, by a woman who spends, spends, spends in places still forbidden to ordinary Chinese, and by a woman who makes her living overseeing other women in cages. I felt like slapping her for the look on Frank's face — like he had been slapped. Instead, I relied on that tried and true method of non-confrontation: I fled.

Most of the group headed for the museum nearby to spend an hour or two before meeting back at the bus for the ride to the airport. Kay and I decided to go for an aimless walk, instead. But after a block or two of that, Kay changed her mind and decided that she, too, wanted to see the museum. Once again, I was left alone on the streets of Shanghai, feeling better and better. I've fallen in love with this city.

I snapped a picture of five old men and an old woman sitting around a makeshift table playing cards in an alley. They were so intent on their game, the flash of my camera startled them, and they turned toward me and laughed. On the wall of the alley was Chinese graffiti. I kept walking, and found myself in a Chinese shopping district with narrow little streets crisscrossing everywhere, so that I felt lost after ten minutes of browsing in bookshops and music shops (violins, mandolins, and other strange-looking long-necked stringed instruments), hardware stores and candy stores. I saw only Chinese people.

Note the graffiti on the wall above these card players in a Shanghai alley

But I was not really lost. When I turned up one tiny lane, I bumped into Jon and Anne on their way to some garden they knew of, so I joined them, despite having seen more gardens by now than you could shake a bamboo stick at. (In the 11th grade, my best friend was Michael Amthor, a German exchange student who always practiced before taking up an invitation: "Oh, vat a be-utiful gahden!") In fact, this was the nicest garden we've seen so far — as much because of our being the only non-Chinese in the place as for its unique beauty.

The garden is enclosed by a wall, which is actually two huge bronze dragons meeting together at the entrance, hideous face to hideous face.

Their mouths are open, revealing two rows of sharpened white teeth (stone? ivory?). Wire smoke curls out of their nostrils like serpents. Their bodies seem to writhe along the wall in hundreds of regular coils. Outside the wall are numerous temples and pagodas surrounding a large carp pond. The corners of the roofs come to long, upturned points, like the fingernails of a Balinese dancer. Stone elephants stand watch at the four corners. A man stood next to a stone railing at the pond, fishing with a bamboo pole. A young couple tried to retrieve a small rowboat with a stick. Behind them, a temple was being renovated, and a massive bamboo scaffolding masked its façade.

Inside the dragon walls, Chinese couples took photos of each other standing in front of romantic ponds that are here and there. The grounds rise precipitously, giving climbers a panoramic view of the extent of the garden compound and the city beyond. I posed for a photo in front of a great Chinese temple door with a hand-carved wooden lattice window. To reach the door, you must pass through a stone archway. Ann took my picture, then pointed at the window behind me. I looked in time to see a woman's face mysteriously disappear behind a white curtain. We never learned who she was or what she was doing there.

Temple under renovation surrounded by ubiquitous bamboo scaffolding

We moved to another temple, and I stood in front of another door, which magically opened. As in a movie an old man beckoned and we entered into what appeared to be his private residence. Just a few steps inside the doorway, he showed us his bonsais, lovingly dwarfed and tended on a shelf just above a fittingly miniature bronze dragon. He offered us tea. This was a personal tour, not on the tourist trail, and we felt both honored and somewhat taken aback by the gesture.

It was time to go, to rejoin our colleagues, to board the bus that would take us to the place that would take us away from this magnificent city. It was a sad moment.

And so here we are, at another depot, ready to go again, to depart, to arrive. People are pressing around Ms. Liu to have their picture taken with her. She has been a fine guide. (She guided the Shanghai Acrobat Troop on its American tour several years ago. But, before that, she spent twelve years banished to rural China, the price of intellectualism during the Cultural Revolution.)

We are seasoned travelers by now. Those of us who are afraid of flying (I, for one, like to do all my flying while securely on the ground) are not more afraid because we are flying in China, I keep telling myself. We have done it before. We're about to do it again.

•••••••••••••••••••••••••••••••••••••••

En route to Guangzhou: Shanghai Prison

After the "No Smoking" light went out (a signal to me not to light up, but to look deliberately at my sweaty palms and laugh), I gazed out the window. We are being borne through the air on a Chinese jet, in Chinese airspace, overflying the Chinese mainland! I hope John Foster Dulles is turning in his grave. I violated one of the few explicit prohibitions; I snapped a photo from the air, an absolute no-no, but I couldn't resist the bright seam of light that is streaming through the dark clouds above, spreading like the ribs of a sandalwood fan on the orange and brown cotton candy clouds below.

Morning sun spreads like the ribs of a sandalwood fan

But back to yesterday's prison visit. The Shanghai Prison is huge, old, barbaric-looking, and governed by the rule of silence. I reached out to one prisoner who took my hand for the briefest moment, a moment that not only breached all the rules of his imprisonment, risking who knows what retaliation, but also all the walls of our own creation, those we impose on ourselves and those imposed by others, to keep us from touching. It was, at least for me, an overwhelming moment.

Men and women — 250 of the 2800 prisoners are women — worked silently at their sewing machines, most not even looking up as we passed. A dark, warm, rain fell steadily outside, the first since leaving the U.S.

The place was built by the British back in 1911, and it is in that style — tiers of cells radiate out from a central guard station. Its history parallels 20th Century colonialism. It has been run by the British, the Japanese, the Chinese Nationalists and now the Chinese Communists.

Although it is much bigger than the Beijing Prison, its cells are much smaller.

Two prisoners share a 5'x9' cell (even the Warren Burger Court would find that hard to swallow), though the cell functions only as a place to sleep. It has no water, no windows, and no amenities of any kind other than a box to store the folded-up bedding in.

We toured the prison, snapping countless pictures of men doing machine work on watch parts (which will be shipped in the boxes that were being repaired by the girls at the work school), and cutting shirt patterns that women prisoners sew together. Afterwards, we were "briefed" by the warden.

He admitted that the rule of silence was enforced as part of the prison regimen, but he couldn't say just how it was related to what goals, other than production goals. He told us that prisoners are to be reformed — Ms. Liu translated his word as "transformed" — through a combination of ideological education and productive labor, the identical tools of transformation being used on people outside the prison.

The ideological education is hard for us to comprehend. According to the rules, no force is allowed, neither corporal punishment nor verbal abuse. What is relied on — and we have heard this at every briefing from the mediation committee to the law faculties — are the "five stresses," which are: morality, manners, hygiene, discipline and decorum, and the "four beautifications": mind, moral character, language and environment. The five stresses and four beautifications (three

French hens, two turtle doves, and a partridge in a pair tree) are responsible for all that is good in China, it seems, and the Gang of Four is responsible for all that is bad.

Kay tried again to get some sense of the national picture, but the warden was an adept bureaucrat, as agreeable as Federal Bureau of Prisons Director, Norm Carlson, and just as duplicitous.

"How many prisons and labor camps are there in China," she asked, "and how many people are held in both?"

"I don't know," he maintained. "Every province and city has one, but I don't know the exact figures."

"Does anyone have these figures?"

"In Beijing, there is such a research organization, but since I work in Shanghai, I don't know what they are."

"Can you estimate," she pleaded.

"No."

But he did tell us that the number of prisoners admitted to his prison in 1980 was 600, that the total discharged was 500, and that there were 2800 prisoners there today. Those three statistics enabled NCCD statistician Jim Galvin, quick as a flash, to calculate that the average sentence length is five years (about twice as long as the average time served in our federal prisons), but that the incarceration rate is about 31 per 100,000 (one-eighth of ours). The trouble is, there is so much we don't know, we can't rely on those figures. For example, we don't know if there are large numbers of people held in pre-trial detention, as there are in American jails.

It wasn't the lack of information that was so depressing, but the walk through the huge Bastille. Mr. Wong, who had never been in a prison before our Beijing visit and — like most Americans — had never thought much about them, walked out with me. With eyes lowered, he said, "That is the last time I will go to a prison."

There are long, very dark corridors that we were forbidden to travel, though we could see the steel doors along either side. The library was housed in a cell — 9'x5' — and had a single prisoner reading at the single desk. I wonder, in fact, if even that isn't a prop for "our foreign friends" since just below the three Chinese characters on the door is the English word, LIBRARY, a sight which inspired dozens of photographs. The infirmary is in another of these tiny cells. In yet another, I peered in through a tiny window to see two prisoners working at something on a desk with one small table lamp, which provided almost no light. They were both young. They looked up at me and smiled.

But it was the lines of men silently bent over work stations — just a few feet in front of the long row of adjacent small cells they occupy — that really got me down. At a long, wide bench, dozens of prisoners sat, side by side, opposite an equal number on the other side. Between the two rows of prisoners facing each other, a long fluorescent lamp stretches the entire length. The layout suggests that these prisoners don't move farther than five feet from their silent cells to their silent work stations. And back.

We had just walked up a twisting and narrow flight of stone stairs when we came into the huge, circular area from which four perpendicular spokes radiate — the tiers of cells and the lines of silent prisoners, each with a bright red and yellow shirt pattern in front of him. At the intersection of the spokes is a wire mesh screen covering a donut hole through which you can see the floor below. Above is another screened donut hole. The white uniformed guards, with red cloth strips on their high collars, swarmed around us, even as Aric and

Kay and I straggled farther and farther behind the main group. (Kay wanted to take a picture of one particularly thug-looking guard at the central control room, but his back was to us. I told her to aim, then shouted, "Hey, Screw!" He immediately turned in our direction, and she got what should be a great picture.)

To anyone who knows the constant, maddening din of American prisons, the total silence of hundreds of captive men at work had its own insane, deafening quality.

As our prison escorts guided the group down the rows of working prisoners from the control room center, I waited. After a minute, I realized that everybody else, miraculously including all the guards, had gone down three of the spokes, leaving me alone to travel down the unguarded one to my right. I started to walk down it. As I did, I caught sight of a young prisoner on the opposite side of the bench from me. He glanced up, darted a look, and then quickly dropped his head back to his work. No other prisoners lifted their eyes from their work.

I kept walking up toward the end of the row where I would turn and walk the narrow aisle between the back wall and the end of the bench, and come back down the other side. He looked up again, furtively, but this time toward the guard station. He saw that the guards were all occupied with the rest of the group, and shot another look toward me. I kept my eyes on him as I turned the corner and started back down. As I came up behind him, I stopped and almost instinctively put my hand out over his left shoulder. He looked again quickly to the right, to make sure he wasn't being observed. (I had already set Kay the task of look-out).

Then he turned his head and looked up at me, reached out and took my hand. He squeezed, just for a second, then let go. He never looked up again.

June 11, Guangzhou, 1:30 a.m.

It seems like I've written a dozen times today. Actually, it's tomorrow, but since I haven't gone to bed from yesterday yet, it's still today. If that makes sense.

We were met here by two local guides, again. They are both young and very attractive women, and Judge Lane is in heaven.

So far, though, they are the only attractive things about this depressing place. We are in a 32-story hotel, built especially for tourists (including many Hong Kong Chinese tourists). It's the pits in every way. First of all, it looks like it was built by an architectural collective — no two rooms are alike, except that all are grotesque. In some rooms, exposed wire pokes out of holes in the ceiling. Doug and I feel cheated because we got the holes but without the exposed wires. Most of the rooms have their very own cockroaches. There were rats downstairs in the cavernous lobby, and the food, if tonight's fare was representative, is so bad that even I can't eat it!

The Bruders' room is the prize possession, and will obviously be the party center. Its heavy red simulated velvet drapes give it the feeling of a San Francisco whorehouse at the turn of the 19th Century.

But even more depressing than the hotel is the mood of the group. We've just come from a bitter meeting with people yelling and screaming at each other about a variety of things. Chief among them is the sense by many members of the group that the Chinese are not giving our demands the weight they deserve, reprising the complaints they brought to the Ministry of Justice very early in the tour. Specifically, our group "leaders" are still trying to figure out a way to wangle a meeting with the Ministry of Public Security.

It is not just that there are only two days left in China that makes this agenda item seem far-fetched. For some reason, these pampered Americans think their stature should be enough to persuade the Chinese secret (and not so secret) police to open their doors and allow themselves to be graced by our visit. But the arrogance of their self-importance was not all that had me shaking my head in disbelief, if not disgust. There was also implied racism. Bill Josephson, who would never expect the Russian KGB to grant an audience to a bunch of American lawyers and federal judges is, nevertheless, sure he can trick the Chinese into granting just such a meeting. I say "trick" because tonight he referred to an unplayed card up his sleeve, a secret plan for gaining admittance into their inner sanctum.

In fact, I think in Bill Josephson, we have created a monster. Actually, we have only fed a monster that was created long ago. Bill is brilliant, there is no question about that. But in his know-it-all way, he has managed to get the rest of us to defer more and more to his judgments. Plus, Dinni already relied on him to a very large degree even before this trip began. Of course, it is good to defer to someone who knows the history of the Chinese criminal code development, or the growing cycle of rice — when you want information about the criminal code or the rice growing cycle. But we defer to him even in matters of personal judgment having little or nothing to do with factual information — and by now, Bill expects and demands deference to his views. Frankly, I think his personal judgments have often been remarkably shallow.

One example occurred at tonight's meeting. I tried to convey the poignancy of the Shanghai prisoner risking — what? — to take my hand. What to me was a significant event, worthy of our discussion on many levels, was to Bill something trivial to snicker at. He dismissed the subject with a knowing, "So what? So you met a prisoner who liked your hand." His unmistakable leering smile implied a sexual motivation, which, apparently, was enough to prevent any discussion from taking place. His sexual inference, though, if true, would be as significant — in a country where "homosexuality does not exist" — as the defiance of authority his touch implied to me.

What made me angriest of all, though, was not Bill's sneering, dismissive attitude. After all, I might just as easily dismiss the grand pronouncements of the lawyers whom he relies on for his significant insights. No, it is the willingness of the rest of the sheep to go along with his quick judgments. Instead of resenting him for his elitism, an elite among elites, this group laps up his pronouncements as if they had come down to him from Mount Olympus.

Another example of this was his reference to a "secret plan" for getting the Ministry of Public Security to meet with us. In fact, he wasn't talking to the group at all, though he was making a presentation to the group. No, he was talking to Dinni. The fact that we were all there listening was irrelevant. "Don't worry, Dinni. I have a plan that I'll tell you about later. You'll like it." He smiled that smug smile of his. Presumably, such a momentous plot could not be entrusted to the rest of us. And no one said a word. Next topic.

I left the meeting feeling both frustrated and angry at a number of people: Bill Josephson for his smugness, his secret strategies, and his off-hand putdown of my experience at the prison; Dinni for being so incredibly indecisive and helpless, or at least appearing that way; Bob Smith for being just as smug and supercilious as Josephson, and for dismissing everybody's point of view, including Josephson's, as "bullshit;" and me, most of all, for not saying any of this to any of them.

Thank god for Kay. She was even more upset by the meeting than I, if that's possible. We went upstairs to her room, where we sat and talked for about an hour after leaving the meeting, which we did before it was over. I think if Kay weren't along, or Aric (who also left in disgust before the meeting ended), I would feel completely and totally isolated.

It has been a very long day. I'm sure things will look better tomorrow. I can't keep my eyes open any more, so I think I'll go to my "suite," scoot the cockroaches out of my bed, and retire.

Mr. Wong

It is difficult to write what I am feeling right now; it is difficult to know what I am feeling. Kay came to my room a few minutes ago and asked if I would join her in Mr. Wong's room to talk. (I was watering my animal in the bathtub at the time, though, of course, she didn't know that.) This is our next-to-the-last night in China, and tomorrow, everyone will be pressing around him for their good-bye photos and heartfelt gratitude. He has been something extra special for us — and, I know now, we have been something special for him, too, some of us in a good way.

He was alone in his room, writing in his official log. We sat. I gave him a tote bag and T-shirt for his wife and baby, but he tried to turn back the gifts. "No, no Michael," he said with some emotion. "You have already given me so much impression, so good impression. I will think about you for many weeks." He spoke glowingly about both of us for a long time. He said that I understood "Chinese thinking," and that I should have been the group leader (can you imagine?), and not Dinni, because "she is not a good leader." Immediately after this pronouncement, he swore Kay and me to secrecy for his indiscreet honesty. He spoke again about my speech at the Chinese Middle School in Wuxi, saying that it had left a lasting impression on the students and teachers, alike, but that it was too short.

It was an embarrassing, but very touching tribute, which has left me with that proverbial lump in my throat, and glowing with warmth. "My tears are falling like rain," one of my wonderful 16-year-old students in Malaysia, Lim Nyun Chung, used to describe this feeling. And, though my tears are not falling like rain, my eyes continue to fill and spill. It is a true comfort to know that Kay and I have touched him in a way that makes him comfortable and open with us, enough to feel free to criticize our fellow Americans, to trust that the bonds of our new friendship are stronger than the bonds of nationality. And, because he has touched us so deeply, we are honored by the trust.

Earlier today, during the question and answer session, which followed a meeting with the lawyers from the Guangzhou Legal Advisory Office, the bitter discussion of the night before surfaced. Various people expressed their anger and disappointment with the arrangements for this trip, saying that we should have been treated better, that we should have been allowed to visit a labor camp, etc. It was the discussion of the night before in the form of now well-practiced questions and statements.

Pearl West's biting attack was the distillation of the group's dissatisfaction: "I am Pearl West, head of the California Youth Authority, and if any of you or your countrymen want to visit any of my facilities, you can do so on five minutes' notice!" (I challenge any American reading this to call her bluff on this claim!) Her voice bristled with righteous indignation. Variations of that sentiment were echoed by a number of other people, all of whom had taken part in the primal therapy of the night before.

Mr. Wong, who was sitting next to me during the meeting, fidgeted more and more uncomfortably until, finally, unable to hold it any longer, he leaned over and whispered, "What are they saying? Do they think we haven't given them all they wanted? Do they think they deserve more? They have seen more than most other groups ever see, and they are not happy?" His voice was tight, and he was clearly both angry and insulted. I passed him a note that said the people expressing their rehearsed anger were as insulting to me and Kay and some others, as they were to him, which didn't pacify him in the least. He had fire in his eyes when he left the room.

Then, tonight in his room, he put it exactly right. "Who do these people think they are," he asked Kay and me. "Do they think they're more important than your Senators who have come, or your judges from the Supreme Court? We have taken them around, and they saw no more than you. Do they think they are so important that everything must be done because they ask that it be done?"

Yes, Kay and I had to agree, they do think they are that important.

Except for the acrimonious ending to the Legal Advisory Office meeting, the substance of the meeting itself was pretty uneventful. The only important thing I remember learning — and I took copious notes for further reference, if I need further reference — is that there is no difference between a labor camp and a prison, except in the kind of labor demanded — farm work in the rural labor camps and industrial work in the urban prisons. It's possible, of course, that rural prisoners also do farm work (most Chinese prisons are located in the countryside, like most Chinese people). Indeed, there is a distinct possibility that I missed some significant details at this meeting. My brain is saturated with lawyer talk, and I have a very low saturation point.

After the meeting, we took a city-wide bus tour, which has put me in a quandary about tomorrow. The morning is taken up with a visit to a nearby commune, which would leave me virtually no time to explore this city. So, I'm leaning toward skipping the commune and taking a walk instead. But that is subject to change.

The bus tour was not very impressive. We ended up at a trade fare where companies loudly hawked their wares as they might in a capitalist trade fare. It was so terrible that I walked out almost immediately, and took a short walk around a very long block. It, too, was uneventful, though I noted that the street vendors are much more aggressive here than they have been elsewhere. It's as if the closer we get to capitalism's domain, the more influence it exerts on people's behavior, like a magnet pulling on a line of iron filings.

There was one semi event on the bus tour. As the bus turned from one road to another, someone spotted a field of sheep, chickens, and a few water buffalo. Pebble yelled for the bus driver to stop, and this group of squealing, snap-happy American tourists, dashed across the street, totally unmindful of traffic (which, this being China, was light enough not to endanger their lives), to take pictures of the barnyard scene. It was like a group of city slickers on their first weekend in the country. Carl Berry, the Green Haven Prison associate warden, almost got gored by a buffalo that, apparently, had religious scruples against being photographed.

But dinner was eventful — and funny.

I was invited to join the vegetarians for dinner at a restaurant they had discovered. Some, like Lynn, are vegetarians by choice. Some, like Steve Kelban, are under doctor's orders. (He discovered he had a heart condition only days before this trip.) I have been thankful many times on this trip that I am not a vegetarian. "You don't know what you're missing" echoes in my mind's ear as my eating companions pass the leftovers for me to finish. That was my father's constant refrain to me, as a child who ate almost nothing but hamburgers and hot dogs. "You don't know what you're missing," he'd say, gnawing on a pork rib. At the time, I thought I knew exactly what I was missing. (Chinese food? Yecchhh! Green salad? It makes me sick! Roast beef and potatoes for dinner? Uggghh! Stew, again!) I was quite content to let my father, and the other omnivores in my family, eat those terrible concoctions, and leave me in peace to eat my hot dog.

Ah, how things have changed. As the omnivore I have become, I feel most sorry for Steve, since he has been a meat eater until only recently, and has not given it up by choice.

But how, you may well wonder, would I get an invitation to dinner from the likes of Steve and his lovely wife, Ellen, my nemesis, or even Lynn, whom I have known for much longer? How, indeed! As it happens, before I got my invitation, they had already invited Kay and Aric, who asked that I be asked. And so I was.

••••••••••••••••••••••••••••••••••

The Vegetarian Restaurant

There were nine of us. We couldn't get a taxi from the hotel, so we bargained with the hotel's tour bus driver, who agreed to take us into town, but not to wait for us. Ellen had the name of the restaurant written on a piece of paper, and had one of the local guides call ahead and make reservations for us. On the way there, Lynn told us at least half a dozen times to let Ellen do the ordering. "She knows what she's doing," Lynn assured us, "so let her do the talking. She knows what she's doing, so no one talk but her," she kept saying, looking directly at this no one. Since I am the only one who speaks even a word of Chinese, I didn't have any doubt who the message was meant for — or, that it had originated with Ellen.

When we got to the restaurant, we were ushered upstairs into our own private dining room. There were no other westerners in sight, though, so it was a promising beginning. We were seated, and a thin, middle-aged woman came to our table to take our orders. Ellen was ready. She pointed to her English-Chinese phrase book where there were pictures of various animals, and, said, "*Bu* beef, *bu* pork, *bu* chicken" as she pointed to each of the corresponding animals on the page.

I almost laughed out loud, but lowered my head instead and even succeeded in stifling a smile. "Bu" is the Chinese adverbial negative that modifies verbs. It might be translated as "do not." So, you would say, for example, "*Wa bu chi*" '— I don't want to eat. Or, more to the point, "*Wa-men bu chi rou*" — We don't want meat. I knew this, of course, and could have assisted, but maliciously, I kept Lynn's counsel. I didn't open my mouth, except, finally, to laugh. Even her husband Steve was laughing by now. No matter how she tried, the waitress just couldn't understand Ellen's attempts to order an all-vegetarian dinner. Various other people, not including me, chimed in — in clear, slow, cadenced English.

Finally, after what seemed like an embarrassingly long time, the poor woman suddenly seemed to get it. Her eyes looked like the comic book version of a light dawning, and she surveyed each of us incredulously. Then, in English, but in very distinct syllables, she asked, "Only vegetables?" It came out as "Own-lee-veg-a-tabulls?" Her voice rose on each of the final four tones, as if to punctuate her question with an exclamation mark. Through guffaws, we nodded assent. She quickly informed us that we had the wrong restaurant, wrote down the address of a vegetarian restaurant, and dispatched one of her helpers, perhaps her son, to walk us the four blocks to the place.

We were suitably embarrassed when we got there, but our former waitress had called ahead, spurring the proprietors of this establishment to action. Again, we were led into our own dining room. This time, a handwritten menu, the ink of the calligraphy still drying, was in the middle of the table. It was beautiful, and before we had sat down, Ellen grabbed it and stuffed it into her oversize purse. Aric and Kay and I shot each other furtive looks, as Ellen quickly explained, "Oh, I have access to a copy machine that reproduces in color. I'll make sure everyone gets a copy..." Everyone remained silent.

Then the meal came, an unbelievable collection of dishes that were both unrecognizable and delicious. One dish that looked exactly like sausage intrigued me so much that I asked our waiter — the owner of the place, I'm pretty sure — what it was. He produced a square of very rough paper, and wrote two large Chinese characters on it, one above the other. Ellen brought out the full menu, and he pointed out the same two characters there. But none of us knew what the characters meant until we got back to the hotel, where Mr. Wong translated them as eggplant. Scrumptious! If you're ever in Canton, may I recommend the Choy Kan Heung Vegetarian Food Shop. And go there with someone who speaks Chinese. Bu Ellen.

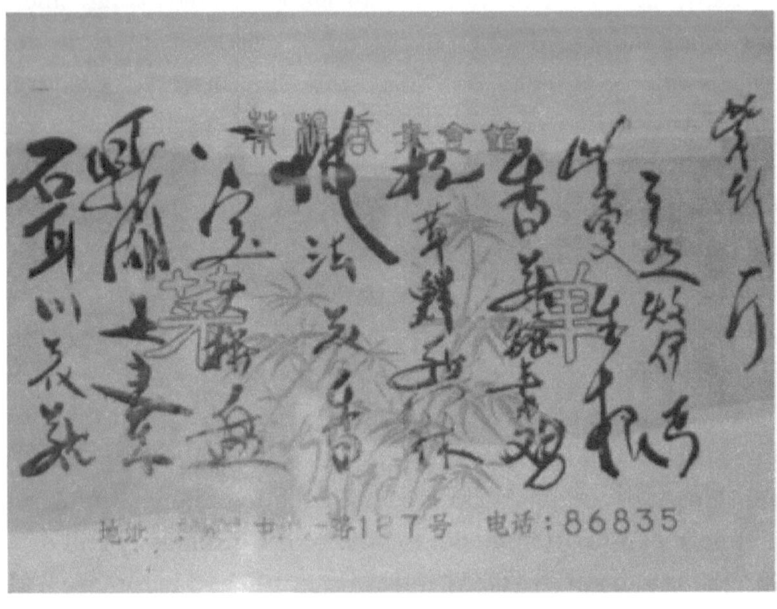

When we finally reached the vegetarian restaurant, this beautiful freshly-written menu was waiting for us.

And now, after that delicious dinner, and our heartwarming talk with Mr. Wong, my mind is moving toward the imminent ending of this journey. I am too full of contradictory impressions to make any reasonable judgments at this point. I am feeling an overwhelming sadness about leaving China. I miss some people at home, of course, but I do not miss work, the city, my apartment, or my bosses. I am not homesick.

Yet, home is where I must go. And very soon.

June 12, Guangzhou, Our Last Night

This is our last night in China. Our last night! Although the hour is late, and I have drunk a lot of the powerful *sake*-like Chinese rice wine, *mao tai*, I want to write about today — as a way to prolong it, if nothing else.

We consumed the *mao tai* tonight, in great quantities, at our final Chinese banquet, hosted by the agency that Mr. Wong works for, the Chinese International Travel Service. Mr. Wong was the guest of honor. It was the kind of boisterous evening you would expect from a group of Americans who have spent the last three weeks together, night and day. The two federal judges got plastered, and sang old Princeton songs. Kay and Rich Friedman from Baltimore left the room to rehearse some ribald number of their own, but couldn't get their act together enough to perform it from beginning to end.

Mr. Wong, his anger from the night before having subsided, made gracious toasts and gratefully accepted the gift that Dinni and "lovely young man" (David Mintz) presented to him on our behalf. It was a Chinese scroll that Dinni had commissioned, expressing our deep thankfulness for all he has done. This cost each of us a few, very well spent, extra yuan.

Wonderful Mr. Wong examines the scroll expressing our gratitude. NCCD Board member, John Bowman, looks on from the left, while tour leader Dinni Gordon looks up from right, and Karamoko Baye looks over Mr. Wong's shoulder.

I snapped pictures of the roast suckling pigs that were carried into the room on large platters. Each table got one! I huddled with Karamoko and Aric to compose our own toasts. With each new toast offered by one of the others, we drank in a little more courage. Aric finally rose unsteadily to his feet and offered this toast: "As the owner of a 400-year-old scroll, I think I am qualified to offer a toast to conspicuous consumption…" This was as mean as he got, which was disappointing. Uncharitably, I had hoped for more, considering that he had told me of the party his fellow Newsday colleagues had thrown for him just before he made the move to Newsweek. He had consumed quite a lot of alcohol then, too, before being called on to toast his good-byes. He rose to his feet, he told me, and said the most gracious things about everyone. Then, as a grand finale, he added, "And, to my boss, that great fat prick..." He doesn't remember anything after that.

For the carnivores among us, the roast suckling pig was as delicious as it was beautiful

Toasting "conspicuous consumption," is Newsweek's Aric Press

There was nothing nearly as rude as that tonight. I was tempted to toast the fact that Bill Josephson's "secret plan" never came to pass, if it ever existed in the first place, but everybody was in a party mood. We could even overlook the drunken speech of Judge B.M. outside the restaurant. He exhorted the small crowd of Chinese who were standing behind the bus to trust their American friends. "Friend," he repeated several times. "Do you understand 'friend'? American friend?" Judge Lane put his arm around the shoulder of his American friend, and guided him into the bus.

Someone — maybe it was me — asked Ms. Chiu, one of our two local guides, whether our behavior wasn't a little bit shocking. "Oh, no," she said, earnestly, "I've guided lots of American groups. I'm used to it."

Before the farewell banquet, we had a full and very fine day. Happily, I resolved my dilemma of yesterday — whether to go to the commune or go walking by having my cake and eating it too. I decided to go the commune in the morning, and then get off the bus downtown on the way back, and walk to the hotel. In fact, quite a number of people got off the bus downtown, but they stayed together, as a group, while I walked off on my own. But I'll get to that walk in a minute.

The commune visit was an official one. That is, it was part of the official People-to-People itinerary, which means that it merited an entry in our own official journal of the trip. Each entry in the journal is the responsibility of a different person, as designated by NCCD's Len Troppin. Today's was the final entry in the journal, and I — who have artfully dodged Len's searching gaze whenever he looks around for a "volunteer" for this task — finally got nabbed. What follows, then, is my official report from the American Legal Delegation visit to the Ta Li People's Commune, (and aren't you glad you don't have to read the entire journal).

"Upon arrival at the Ta Li People's Commune (40 minutes southwest of Guangzhou), we were greeted by Mr. Ling, the Vice-Chairman of the Commune Revolutionary Committee. In a formal briefing session, he delivered the following information about the commune:

"Of the 14 communes in Guangdong Province, Ta Li ranks fourth in size and output. Its population of 70,000 includes 17,000 families. The labor force is divided into 19 production brigades and subdivided into 229 production teams. Ta Li has nearly 10,000 acres (59,000 mu) of arable land. Most of this acreage is devoted to the production of rice; the remainder is used for watermelons, peanuts, sweet potatoes and other vegetables. In addition, the commune raises a diverse collection of farm animals such as pigs, poultry, water buffalo and fish. In 1980, approximately 93,000 pigs were born. Currently, the commune has over 450,000 poultry, 2,000 water buffalo, and 2,000 mu of fish ponds. Ta Li also operates its own grain-producing factory and farm repair workshop.

"In addition to these agricultural enterprises, the commune has a lime factory, cement factory, print shop, and plastic bag and plastic shoe factory.

It also operates a machine parts assembly plant where 7,000 commune members may earn income in addition to their regular jobs.

"Living standards at Ta Li are good. The population is fed with surplus grain, and at the end of the year, each able-bodied member earns between 65 and 1,000 yuan (about $105-$161). Income is distributed according to individual contribution and need. To raise living standards, great stress is being placed on education. The commune has twenty primary schools, several junior middle schools, and one secondary middle school. Health services include three commune hospitals and twenty health centers, which are financed through individual payments from the workers (20 cents per month), and payments from each production team (80 cents for each team member). There are six mobile movie projectors, which tour the commune several times a week showing movies. The more prosperous production teams (and even individuals) have television sets.

"A commune management commission, consisting of 15 members, is charged with the overall management of the commune. Each member of the commission undertakes a different area of responsibility (e.g. environmental protection or public security). Dispute mediation is handled by a committee at the production brigade level, and if this fails, a member of the commission intervenes to arbitrate.

"Theft is the most common crime, though its occurrence is uncommon. If a theft is minor, the matter is handled by issuing a verbal warning to the offender. Major thefts and habitual thieves are turned over to the procurator's office.

"Although families in the countryside are not penalized for having two children, they are still encouraged to have only one. The fact that the average family in Ta Li is more than four people is due not only to extended family units, but also to the legacy before family planning became national policy.

"At the conclusion of our visit, the delegation toured a commune orchard and irrigation system. We then visited a village of nearly 400 workers who were served by the Hao Mei production brigade. After

speaking with several of the workers in their homes, we returned to the main building for a large and very delicious lunch."

That's the official, formal report. Boring, ain't it? Now here's the interesting stuff.

The commune was a wonderful reminder of what it is like to live among and with Chinese people. In fact, it looked like whole sections of my small town in Borneo, where the Chinese organize around family and extended family units instead of around production brigades. I'm sure production is higher here, but the feeling of the two places is almost exactly the same. In both places, the water buffalo stand ankle-deep in the mud of the paddies; the pigs and piglets wallow in their pens; and children run in and out of different homes, tended by all.

As usual, I hung back from the rest of the group and explored a little on my own. That meant a game of hide-and-seek with a five-year-old boy with a water pistol. I came upon an old man tossing a flat woven basket of grain into the air to separate the wheat from the chaff. He was surrounded by pesky children whom he continually scolded for getting under foot. I walked down narrow alleyways between one and two-story brick houses. I saw one cat, but no dogs.

Ta Li People's Commune. Note the boy in the doorway with the water pistol who shadowed me.

Back with the group, I spoke to Mr. Ling, the revolutionary committee vice chair, about my experiences in Tawau more than a dozen years before. He knew some Hakka, and I was able to call up a phrase or two from my memory.

When my group went into the home of one of the Ta Li residents (we had broken into two groups, each doing the same things in different places), I sat outside the house on the steps and played with a growing group of growing children. After about twenty minutes, when most of my fellow Americans had wandered out, I went in. The room was decorated in a way that reminded me of my student Ah Kiong's house on Sin On Road in Tawau. The walls were a collage of family photos, old travel posters, bits and pieces of unmatched wall paper, and an altar dedicated to the memory of various ancestors, some of whose pictures were arranged near it. Red joss sticks were burning on the altar, and there was an offering of an orange and two eggs.

The kitchen was small. On a table in the center was an ancient fire-heated rice cooker and a large wooden vat with a heavy wooden lid, set into a large wooden plank that served as both cutting board and table. There was one clear difference between this kitchen and the Malaysian one I was mentally comparing it with.

Here, next to the old rice cooker, was an electric one, plugged into an outlet in the wall behind the table. In Ah Kiong's house, there was no electricity.

The electric rice cooker at left is next to the old-fashioned wooden version in this commune resident's kitchen.

When I went into the living room, most of the Americans had left. But Aric and Kay and the Bruders were still there, questioning a young Chinese mother who held court in the middle of the room. While they kept tossing out questions ("How much does your husband make? How long did you have to wait for this house? Do you want other things?"), the woman balanced a baby, moving him from one knee to another, as she answered.

I didn't hesitate. I walked up to her and put my arms out to take the baby, who immediately came to me. The young mother smiled gratefully, and continued answering questions. As she did, this very beautiful, fat-faced one-year-old and I played. As we both gurgled and laughed, I was transported back to Tawau, tossing one-year-old Lee Siu Ming over my head and laughing.

When we went back to the main building for lunch, we were served by teenaged girls who giggled when they saw us. Various thoughtful members of the group passed the fish heads to Len Troppin who savored them, a true Chinese delicacy that I, uncharacteristically, do not eat. All in all, it was another very enjoyable meal.

Farm machinery at the Ta Li People's Commune. Tour bus in background.

The bus dropped us off right downtown, and I immediately separated myself from the horde (not to say "herd") who walked into the poster shop. (I had already bought my Mao — and Stalin! — posters in Beijing.) I really had no notion of where I was going, or even how I would get back to the hotel, but I set off.

I walked for nearly three hours, and the most amazing thing about it is that I saw not a single western face in that time. I walked down wide dirt roads with shops and houses on both sides. I browsed in a number of shops, and bought a wonderful pointed bamboo hat for one yuan and 22 fen. I had a cup of tea from a street vendor. Once, when I turned a corner, two ten-year-old girls coming towards me did a classic double-take, and then covered their eyes with their hands. Coincidentally, just yesterday I read in <u>China Men</u>, the extraordinary book by Maxine Hong Kingston, that when she was growing up in Stockton, they would cover their eyes as children when suddenly confronted with a western face so that the "*kui*" (ghost or devil) would not see them. But this devil saw them anyway, and smiled.

My favorite street was a very narrow lane with animal dealers along both sides. Some of the animals were for food — the turtles, for example — and some for pets. Or, at least I want to believe they were for pets. What else would owls be for, or an animal that looks like a Chinese armadillo? There were birds and frogs, monkeys and eels, owls and chickens. There were cages of every size and description.

Naturally, I do know the word for "snake" in Chinese. It's *sah*. In Malaysia, my Chinese students derived enormous pleasure by greeting me each day, "Good morning, Sah." Using the word now, I kept asking if anyone had one. Finally, one young man beckoned for me to follow him, which I did, through a coffee shop and into a small courtyard, where he made clear he wanted me to help him transfer the *sah* from a large cloth bag into an even larger one. It took both of us to lift the ten-foot python, a thick mass of wriggling coils, out of one bag and then to wrestle it into another. I didn't buy it. No sah,!

And finally, I looked for a way to get back to the hotel so I wouldn't miss the feast. Mr. Wong had written down its name and address for me, but I had no idea how to catch a bus. I just kept walking toward what appeared to be the commercial center of Canton. To my great surprise, even astonishment, I was able to spot a taxi and flag it down.

Rush-hour traffic — what seemed like millions of walkers, bicycles and more cars and buses than I had seen in any other Chinese city — made it slow going, but I didn't mind. The taxi driver, a woman, seemed unsurprised and unconcerned that her fare was a *kui*. In fact, despite being the only westerner in three hours of walking, I attracted very little of the kind of attention our presence has generated almost everywhere else. Except for the snake transfer, which attracts a crowd anywhere, and the two lovely little girls who covered their eyes, nothing

I did seemed worthy of a second look by the multitude of Chinese I passed all afternoon. Whether that is due to its proximity to Hong Kong or its familiarity with the west through television, I can't say. I can say, however, that it was fine with me.

Anyway, by the time I got back to the hotel, I had only about half an hour to rest, water my snake, and get ready to go again. Ah, the life of the leisure class.

And now, after all that, it is very late, and I am very tired. It is unsettling to think about tomorrow. In just a few hours, China will be a memory. I wish there were some way of holding back the dawn.

Good night, Mr. Wong.

June 13, Hong Kong

It's over.

That first walk through Narita, into the stationery store to buy this writing paper, and then to the temple to write the first reflection is like a memory from another age. Already, China shimmers in glimpsed shards of memory. It's as if it all took place in the dream world, full of good fairies and bad, ancient and future competing for survival.

When I left my room this morning for the last time (and good riddance to that room), I found Aric sitting by the elevator with his head in his hands, as if he feared it would fall off if he let it go. His conspicuous consumption of the night before had come up some time in the middle of the night, and he looked like shit.

After breakfast, which nobody ate, we boarded the bus for the last time and were taken to the train station. Our dear Mr. Wong had left earlier for the airport to return to Beijing.

The train, like all the others, was first-class and luxuriously comfortable. Most of us just watched as China slipped away. Rice paddies stretched off in both directions until they met the imposing mountains rising up on all sides. Rivers and irrigation canals paralleled the tracks. A tiny cemetery, perhaps belonging to a single family, could be seen on a small knoll overlooking a lake.

After a while, people started moving around. Kay, who was sitting next to me, asked if I would change places with Steve Kelban so that she could talk about NCCD's future with him. As Program Officer, Kelban advises Ken Schoen, the former Corrections Commissioner of Minnesota who now runs the Edna McConnell Clark Foundation, which funds the most progressive non-profits in the world of corrections, like the NCCD. Kay came back a short time later disgusted by his smug certainties and his shallow understanding, well camouflaged by his little-boy cuteness and charm. She cited his critique of Milt Rector as an example of his inexperienced advocacy of style over substance.

"What NCCD needs is a person who isn't so dogmatic and uncompromising at its helm," he lectured Kay. It wasn't necessary to tell her, after that, that he had never actually seen or heard Milt Rector testify. Rector, of course, is the legendary executive director of NCCD, a towering model of rationality, clarity and decency. But to this self-important lawyer, barely out of law school but making a fortune, what was needed was someone a little snappier, someone with pizzazz, as if that would overcome the irrationality that characterizes so much of what passes for correctional policy:

Is it rational to spend such budget crushing amounts on after-the-fact "corrections," while spending almost nothing to ameliorate poverty and debilitating social conditions that might prevent or reduce criminal behavior in the first place?

Is it rational to declare war on drugs, ratcheting up the length of prison sentences to a degree that shocks the rest of the world (especially the western world, which treats drug addiction as a public health challenge rather than a criminal justice challenge)?

Is it rational to use this self-declared war on drugs to ensnare a hugely disproportionate number of young Black and Brown men into our net of criminal justice controls, truncating their futures while doing nothing to stem America's insatiable appetite for illegal drugs?

Is it rational to stuff our prisons until they hold twice or more of their design capacity, leaving them bursting at the seams and teeming with violence?

Is it rational to hold ourselves up as "the land of the free" when we imprison more people, per capita, than any nation on earth, and when more than half of those are there for non-violent offenses?

Is it rational for the political class to immunize itself from the charge of "soft on crime" by doubling and tripling the length of prison sentences, further aggravating an already crushingly expensive and bloated prison empire?

Is it rational to call this industry "corrections" at all, when it does so little to correct and so much to exacerbate anti-social behavior? (Or, is "correcting behavior" not the real goal of this job-generating growth industry?)

Is it rational to rely on the infallibility of a system constructed by people to determine who among us is no longer fit to live?

Indeed, how rational is it to kill people to teach people that killing people is wrong, leaving us in the company of such "modern" executioners as Cuba, Iran and, of course, China?

That's the kind of Kroll rant that guarantees I will never get a grant from Edna McConnell Clark, but Milt Rector? He is the person you would invent to give your testimony, if he did not already exist — cool, courtly, eminently reasonable, knowledgeable and unflappable — my exact opposite.

●●

When we got to the border, the police state reared its ugly symbolic head. There were double cyclone fences, topped with rolling coils of barbed wire and razor ribbon, which extended as far as the eye could see. Armed soldiers patrolled the area. Our train stood on a siding for some minutes next to another train. I could see an old Chinese woman through my curtained window, waiting patiently for her papers to be inspected.

And then into Hong Kong. This is where the dream world ends.

Having been here before, I watched the faces of my fellow travelers as more and more of this city unfolded. Total incredulity. Hong Kong is as much our world as theirs, unleashed and wicked, like Sodom and Gomorrah. Honky-tonk and neon. Vendors offering knock-off watches, on-the-spot tailoring services, their sisters. Bumper-to-bumper traffic, coughing exhaust fumes into the air. Hillside shanty towns that are still called "temporary," as they were when they were first erected for the flood of refugees that came after the Communist victory in 1949.

New York's Lindy's Restaurant and Delicatessen next to a tiny Chinese food shop called Lin Thai's, with slabs of pork and dripping roast ducks hanging in the window. Lovers strolling through the streets and unabashedly kissing in the parks.

Lights glittering through the night.

Hong Kong is in two parts, the Kowloon Peninsula on the mainland, and Hong Kong Island just across Victoria Harbor. Our hotel, the Miramar in the heart of Kowloon's glitter, has a console panel between the beds that allows guests to open and close the curtains automatically. We have no room keys. Instead, we insert a plastic card into a slot outside the door, which trips a computer lock, and the door clicks open. Bellhops wear pill-box hats, like in the Philip Morris commercial.

We took a cruise this evening. It was a thoroughly tourist affair, complete with free booze and a sleazy photographer who snapped away, despite my repeated protestations that I intended to buy nothing. (I kept expecting him to offer me dirty post cards.)

Through the congested waters we cruised, past tiny boats and huge yachts, around a promontory on the east side of Hong Kong Island into Aberdeen Harbor, famous for its floating restaurants and its Chinese junks, where whole families are born and die without ever leaving the water. We ate at one of the floating restaurants, a garish boat festooned with lights that can be seen for miles. Inside, the place is so jammed with tourists, it is difficult for the waiters to make their way between the tables. The tables themselves are so close together that you are almost butt-to-butt with the person sitting at the table behind you (or, behind-to-behind with the person at the table that abuts you). In the center of the room is a dragon whose neon eyes and nostrils compete for attention with the neon breasts of the mermaid on the ceiling. The din is deafening, a Babel of voices.

Hong Kong is a rude reminder of the frenetic world that we are returning to, but still, I love the decadence of this moneyed city.

June 14, Hong Kong: My Shameful Meltdown

I had a strange, deranged dream last night that probably means the tension I so visibly shed as I traveled from Washington is about to grip me again, as I prepare to return.

I was in a crowd of people. Somebody was telling me that we had just been sentenced to a year in prison for draft evasion. Kay kept asking, "Has anyone got a nickel? I have to make a phone call." The man who was telling us to get ready for our imminent imprisonment pointed across the street to some fast food place, a Chicken Delight, I think, where Kay could presumably make her call — assuming she ever got the nickel she so desperately appealed for. She tried to cross the street, but oncoming buses and bicycles impeded her progress, and she had to step back onto the curb. Meanwhile, I just kept thinking two thoughts over and over. First, "Goddamit! I'm 26 years old and I have served this goddamn country!" Then, immediately, "I'm really about to spend the next year living in a prison. I must prepare myself. I must be ready."

But I am not ready. I wish, truly wish, that I were traveling east from here and not west. No, no. That's not right. I am traveling east from here, and not west.

What I meant to say is that I wish I were traveling west from here to the East instead of east from here to the West.

I woke up early this morning and took my usual stroll. About half a mile from the hotel, I found the kind of open market I have found in every Chinese city I've visited — the part of the city that remains the most distinctly Chinese, no matter how modern the buildings. On streets blocked to traffic, throngs of Chinese people, almost all women and children, dressed in colorful but baggy trousers with short-sleeved pajama tops, made their way among tin-covered stalls and uncovered wicker baskets. The profusion of fruit and vegetables gave the early morning air a deliciously distinct aroma that, though I can't identify, still conjures previous walks through similar markets in Singapore and Kuala Lumpur.

I bought a bunch of rambutan, a red-skinned fruit covered with hair-like fibers. (*Rambut* means "hair" in Malay, and rambutan is everywhere in Malaysia, where I first discovered it.) When you peel the skin — more like a soft pod — it yields a deliciously sweet lychee-like pulp around a small brown seed. I snacked as I walked. I saw one woman in black Viet Cong pajamas, flossing the teeth of another woman, whose face was powder white. I saw three young men quickly dismantle their street display of clothes and disappear into the crowd, as a couple of uniformed policemen approached.

Early morning Hong Kong street market

Then I walked back to the hotel for breakfast, past the Chinese medicine shops, past the goldsmiths and tailors, past the golden arches of McDonald's.

I had already decided to spend my last day in Asia just walking. Tonight's final banquet (final final banquet) is our last group activity. Most everybody leaves tomorrow for Seattle, while Kay and I are flying to Honolulu — no extra charge for R&R.

This morning, while everybody gathered downstairs to board yet another bus for yet another city tour, I tarried in my room so as to miss the pre-boarding socializing. But when I went downstairs, they were still there, which led to a guilt producing run-in with Len Troppin, the last person I would want to offend, though offend him I surely did. As I walked past him, he grabbed my arm and said he wanted $3 from everybody so we could buy a nice gift for Dinni. Why this should have been the last straw for this camel's back, I can't say, but it was. I told him he could have the money, of course, but that I resented it, and not just a little. Understandably taken aback, he said, "Look, you're not going to get away with that without an explanation!"

"All right," I said, "You want an explanation? The class of people on this tour doesn't understand that $3 for this and $5 for that is significant to some of us. I figure the $4,000 I paid for this trip should have covered the costs of good-bye and thank-you presents." And I walked out, leaving unsaid what I was really thinking, which is that a $100 gift is an extravagance that is not deserved by our fearless leader, whose free trip, by virtue of being the leader, should be payment enough.

But even without saying it, Len already looked shocked and hurt by my outburst. I think, for anyone who truly knows me, which Len does not, this unseemly temper tantrum would not be a surprise. I'd kept these thoughts confined to paper for too long. The thing is, how much easier it would have been to cough up the three bucks, and borne my grudge in silence. And how slow I am to learn this lesson.

Anyway, it's later now. They are touring the city on wheels, while I am about to set out on foot to explore, again, this fragrant harbor (*heung kong*) that is Hong Kong.

The Star Ferry and Peninsula Hotel

I took the Star Ferry across Victoria Harbor to Hong Kong Island after my flap with Len this morning. At 20 cents in each direction, it is a marvel of mass transportation. To get to the ferry terminal from our hotel on Nathan Road, the biggest and busiest thoroughfare on the Kowloon side of the harbor, you have to walk past the Peninsula Hotel, one of the most beautiful and gracious Colonial-era hotels still standing. Like the similarly impressive Raffles Hotel in Singapore, it was built in a different age when Brittania ruled the waves. Guarded by a pair of huge bronze lions, it is a magnificent testament to tea-time — a genteel setting for the refined English to escape the din of the Chinese commercial world outside, and to rest from a day's toil of plundering the resources of the Colony, while providing a British Civil Service system in exchange. It is the architectural embodiment of elegance.

A dozen years earlier, I had had a psychic experience at the Peninsula. I had awakened early at my $5-a-night Chinese hotel with the very strong impression, almost a certainty, that I would meet somebody I knew that day. I even told the person I was traveling with at the time of my premonition. Later that morning, we bumped into a man we both knew from Malaysia. My friend marveled at my predictive powers, but I said, "No, that isn't it. I still have the feeling."

Hours later, having forgotten all about it, I wandered into the Peninsula for the first time, feeling like a proper expatriated Englishman, when — lo and behold — there were two friends of mine whom I hadn't seen since Peace Corps training four years earlier. While sipping tea in the spacious and gracious sitting room of my friends' outrageously expensive Peninsula Hotel room, reason told me it was coincidence, and not telepathic communication, that led me here. But I was not yet willing to wake from the unreality of this adventure, and so, cynic though I am, I contemplated the mysteries of the untapped mind, as I bit into my second scone.

Today, though, I didn't have tea in one of those posh rooms. Instead, Aric and I, joined by Connecticut Corrections' Department Deputy, Larry Albert and his wife Marilyn (whose full mouth of braces always makes her look like a high school cheerleader to me), had coffee in the grand pillared lobby downstairs.

This was after I took Aric back with me to Hong Kong Island across the harbor from the Peninsula. I had spent the morning on the island, by myself, wandering up the steep, narrow streets that were just coming alive at that hour. My unfailing sense of the reptilian led me to the back of a shop where baskets were piled high, filled with writhing rat snakes — long, green slender animals with red heads. A boy of about sixteen was removing them, one by one, holding a tail down with his foot, and then slitting them up the side and dumping the squirming fresh meat into a large bucket (so reminiscent of that first day in Narita, Japan, where a bucket of eels suffered the same fate). The street around him looked like the carnage left after a gangland slaying, once the bodies have been removed. For a small sum, I liberated one of the condemned creatures, and stuffed it into my shoulder bag.

At the corner of the same street was a small hardware and basket store.

Scores of baskets hung from the eaves of the shop, and many more were stacked inside. Two baskets immediately caught my eye. The first, hanging outside the shop, was a huge wicker hamper, about two feet long and a foot and a half deep and wide. Two large flaps fold over each other to make the lid, which is held down by a piece of bamboo slid between two wicker loops poking through holes in the top flap. The double wicker handles are attached to thongs that are knotted artfully to the basket itself. An inch-wide border of alternating green and pink wicker surrounds the top and the bottom. I had to have it (which is exactly what Ellen said when she plunked down her 300 yuan for the antique basket she bought in Shanghai).

And I do have it — for the grand sum of $2.50! And that's not all. I also bought a second basket, this one hanging inside the shop. It is a rounded wicker and bamboo cat-carrying basket. I don't have a cat to carry in it, of course, but that's beside the point. (Could it be a snake basket, I wondered.) I couldn't carry both baskets, so I bought the large one first, took it back to the hotel, then bought the second — for less than the first — on my return trip with Aric. You just never know when you might need a wicker cat carrying case.

I returned to the hotel for lunch (to save money) to find the group, returned from their bus tour. Kay and Karamoko, I learned, had also skipped the tour to do their own thing. They had spent the morning drinking at the hotel overlooking the beach at Repulse Bay. Aric, who, like everyone else, complained that the tour had been pretty awful, said that he had to go over to the Hong Kong side to look up his father-in-law at a hotel there. I prevailed on him to let me tag along, on the promise that I would take him to the wicker basket shop, which I did, so that he could buy a basket, which he did. He also bought a set of wicker serving trays that would have cost more than I could afford at home, but which cost him about ten dollars here. We went to the hotel, but his father-in-law was out.

I confided my secret menagerie to Aric, and swore him to secrecy. He looked mildly shocked — perhaps as much that anyone would want to keep snakes as that I was going to schlep them across the Pacific, and smuggle them into the United States. He asked how I intended to get them out of Hong Kong, much less into the U.S. I told him I trusted the snake-god to guide me safely through my perils.

We caught the ferry back to Kowloon to get ready for the good-bye banquet, where Dinni would get her accolades and her gift, and where I intended to get good and drunk. Which put me in a quandary. A free bar was set up an hour before dinner. By this time, I didn't want to spend any more time with the group than I had to, but I also wanted to get the most out of the drinking arrangements. If I were too early,

I'd have to mingle. If I were too late, I'd miss the booze altogether. A delicate balance. I decided to give myself fifteen minutes to down as many drinks as I could put away in that time.

On the way back to our hotel, Aric and I stopped and had our cup of coffee at the Peninsula with the Alberts. Then, he had to do some final gift buying, and Hong Kong is definitely the place for it. I went back to the hotel, wished that I had some marijuana, and toyed with the idea of wearing my three-piece suit, to shock my fellow travelers with my class. ("You must carry one suit," the People-to-People pre-trip guidelines commanded.) Instead, I wore the beautiful batik shirt I bought earlier this morning in a shop where I had a short conversation in Malay with the Indonesian woman who owns it. ("*Ma'afkan saya, tetapi saya sudah lupa semua bahasa Melayu...*" — I'm really sorry, but I've forgotten all my Malay...)

I watered my growing zoo — the snake with tiger fish eyes, and today's near victim, spared by the beneficent intervention of Michael the Merciful — donned my brand new batik shirt (purchased for a pittance), and made my hesitant way to the Holiday Inn (that is NOT a joke) for our party.

It appeared that everybody was already there. I doubt that I had stepped more than two feet into the room when Ellen rushed up to me and grabbed my hand, like a dear friend, gushing, "Have you seen it yet, Michael? Oh, it's wonderful. Wait 'til you see it." (It occurred to me that she may actually have smoked what I had so recently wished to smoke. Or that I should have gotten to the bar earlier...)

I had no idea what she was talking about, of course, but it didn't matter. Nothing mattered except getting to that free bar. As I made my way, others in the group echoed Ellen's questions: Have you seen it? Do you like it?

At the bar, I ordered a double bourbon and steered in Kay's direction. When she saw me, she smiled in a conspiratorial way, though

I was not part of the conspiracy. "OK, Kay, what is this thing that everybody keeps asking me about?"

"Who told you?" she asked, in mock disappointment. "It was supposed to be a secret." With that, she reached into a brown paper bag and pulled out a little plate, slightly larger than a saucer, and handed it to me. A garish dragon slinks around the white edge of the plate, perhaps in pursuit of the equally garish combination peacock-rooster that scrambles away on the opposite edge. At the top are Chinese characters whose meaning I assume is the same as the English words at the bottom: Hong Kong. In the middle of all this, a smiling picture of me fills the center of the plate, a mass of wind-blown hair in the foreground, with a bit of Hong Kong visible behind me. It is a picture that the sleazy photographer had taken of me on the harbor cruise, the one I would not buy from him. Kay said, "I knew you would never spend money on something like this, so I bought it for you as a surprise."

Kay's gift to me, a souvenir plate of Hong Kong which is visible in the background.

It is the perfect Hong Kong souvenir: tacky, touristy and totally tasteless. I love it. Though it's designed to be exhibited (it comes with a foldable wooden stand), I can hardly wait to stack it high with cashews and pass it around at a party. "Nuts?" I'll suggest. Despite my antipathy for the photographer, it is a really good picture of me.

When I got back to the bar for another double, it was too late. My timing had been terrible. Aric, who swears after his pre Hong Kong hangover that he will never take a drink again, missed the bar altogether by coming in just then, in time for dinner.

We ended up at the only table which still had two empty seats. When we sat down, Judge B.M., sitting across the table from me, leaned over and asked, "How do you like your plate, David?"

And we ate. Not Chinese food. Holiday Inn food. Pork chops. Mind you, I like pork chops. Aric, who keeps a kosher house in Brooklyn but who "isn't a fanatic about it" (meaning, while in China he gave himself dispensation to ignore certain dietary laws) decided to practice re-entry, so I had the pleasure of both his and my pork chops.

And that was about the only pleasure. Unlike the final banquet in China, the party mood tonight seemed forced and phony, people doing what was expected of them when they'd all really rather be somewhere else. After dinner, Len got up and made the expected speech about Dinni's "selfless leadership," and presented her with the $100 token of our esteem — a fancy travel alarm clock! (If I paid $100 for an alarm clock, I'd want it to make my breakfast after it woke me up...)

And then it was over. The end. People stood in small groups and slowly made their way to the door. It had been a contrived last evening of conviviality. China was behind us.

My roommate Doug went off in search of Suzy Wong. Aric and Kay and I walked back toward our hotel, not knowing what else to do. Kay suggested we go into a little Spanish bar she and Karamoko had discovered the night before, but Aric insisted on leaving us at the entrance. "I have to go back to that pen store," he said. "I'm sure I can get that Parker if I just raise my offer slightly..."

Kay and I went in and had a pitcher of beer. We talked some, but not much. We were both thinking about China. It was all beginning to sink in, just the fact of the trip, itself. Reflections have begun, but not real comprehension. Not yet, anyway, if ever.

We walked back to the hotel, past the shop where Aric was still bargaining with the pen merchant, and said good night. And here I am, sitting and writing in an empty hotel room. It feels like I'm waiting for something to happen, but I don't know what. I guess I'm just waiting to go to sleep. Tomorrow is another early start day, to the airport and through Immigration (horrors!), and then to Honolulu and Customs (more horrors!).

It is all so unreal.

June 15, Honolulu, Hawaii

This is it, the last written contribution before I resume my former life. But, sitting here with Kay on the beach at Waimea on Oahu's north shore, I have, through an intense act of sheer will, completely obliterated all thoughts of Washington, D.C., and, most particularly, all thoughts of my Unitarian bosses, who await my reluctant return while practicing their expressions of love for me. (Frankly, I wish they loved me less and liked me more.) But, as I say, there is not the trace of a thought of any of that in my head, obliterated as it is.

Note the date of this entry is the same as yesterday's. Through the miracle of modern technology and aerodynamics, although we woke up twelve hours ago in Hong Kong, where it was June 15th, we have traveled 5,000 miles back in time to the 14th.

I bundled myself into the elevator this morning in Hong Kong, and emerged into the crowded hotel lobby, looking like a bag lady with an affinity for Chinese baskets. I had thought I couldn't possibly schlep my baskets and hats and bags of loot at the same time, but there I was. In fact, there we all were, with our oversize bags, boxes, baskets and baggage, making us look like the most affluent refugees ever to escape from China. We were bussed to the airport, an utter madhouse.

Unlike our departure from China, which was the smoothest, least cumbersome exit I have ever made from any country, leaving Hong Kong requires amazing restraint and patience. I had to return from the immigration section to the ticket section three times to check excess baggage, which must conform exactly to size specifications to carry onboard. Others had to return even more often. It wasn't just things like my baskets, either, but small items like Chinese hats and flutes that stuck out here and there, like unwanted growths, violating one regulation after another.

Finally, though, we were all through the checkpoints and awaiting our flights. The group's plane to Tokyo and Seattle left first, so Kay and

I got to bid everyone farewell, and make the usual empty promises to reunite, to exchange pictures, to compare notes. I was genuinely sorry to say good-bye to Aric, but we are friends now, and our promises to see each other were sincere.

And then we were left alone, among the hundreds of other tourists coming and going. I could feel my two slithery creatures, secure in their own "snake bag" which was secure inside my carry-on flight bag. It had received only a cursory look, to my great relief. (I was sure they would hear my heart pounding, and ask me to open the bag.)

But it was Honolulu's Customs' inspection that I really dreaded. I have that kind of face that invites abuse by customs officials the world over, but nowhere have I been more abused than coming in through Honolulu. Once, in fact, I had to submit to a strip search, even though I wasn't even the passenger arriving in the country, but only meeting a friend who was. But that's another story.

Anyway, we landed in Honolulu and started through customs. It was about ten in the morning, and the customs area was not crowded. I gathered up my baskets and suitcases and bags and got in line, my telltale heart crashing away. Kay, who had less stuff than I, was already in another line. When my turn arrived, I put the baskets and bundles on the conveyer belt and waited for the official, a young Asian woman, to order me to open them up. Which she did in the most agreeable fashion. I had never dealt with such a polite and agreeable customs official at this airport. (Could I have been responsible for such a change? After that full-cavity body search a few years ago, I had written to my Congresswoman, Patsy Mink, who initiated a Congressional investigation of customs personnel in Hawaii. Maybe this was the sweet fruit of that investigation.)

I took out everything she asked to see, while she plied me with a steady stream of questions about China. Living in Honolulu, she knew what to expect from American tourists. "Have we ruined it yet," she asked, excitedly. "Was it fantastic? Did you get to Shanghai? What was the weather like? Could you go anywhere you wanted to?" I was really getting into it with her, enjoying the animated discussion, which I hoped would distract her from my shoulder bag. It didn't. She asked me to open it and hand it to her, which I did. While she poked around in it, she barely took her eyes off me, and our dialogue continued.

Then she found the rice-sack snake bag, which was tied at the top, and took it out. Even as she kept up her barrage of questions, she began untying the knot.

Is this the point where I confess that my bag is full of heroin, I wondered, as the knot came undone? Do I stop her gallantly, before she reaches into the bag, and, with a dramatic flourish, announce the existence of the contraband inside? Do I... Oh, no! Too late! She is reaching into the bag! I am holding my breath!

"Aiiiiaaaaaahhhh," she screams, letting the bag fall to the floor, "There's a snake in there! If it had been alive, it would have bit me!"

"Oh no," I corrected, only faintly aware of the flurry of uniformed officials approaching from several directions, "they are alive, but they're really very gentle. They won't bite you."

"They?" she asked, incredulous. "You mean there's more than one?"

Kay, who was already through her customs inspection, heard the commotion and thought I had been busted for drugs — and wondered idly where I had got them. Then she heard the word "snake" and she knew.

"Oh fuck," she thought, "this is my first trip to Hawaii and I'm going to spend it trying to get Michael out of jail!"

As a couple of officials took me to the office of the State Agricultural Officer, I smiled gamely, and told Kay I'd be right out. She didn't look like she believed me. I didn't believe me, either, even though, to my surprise, pandemonium had not broken out. One of the officials laughingly recalled the time when "Rick opened that bag and that huge python zoomed out the top, remember that?"

After I was ushered politely into the official's office, he sat me down and asked me what kind of snakes they were. I told him I wasn't sure, but that one of them was obviously a rat snake of some kind. Neither one, I assured him, was poisonous and neither was aggressive. He reached into a lower desk drawer and pulled out a five-page list of protected animals, scanning it quickly. There were no Chinese snakes on it. He informed me that the mere possession of snakes, like marijuana, was illegal in Hawaii, which has no snakes indigenous to it. I knew this, of course, since I had lived here (and kept an illicit boa constrictor, until it got away). But I didn't confess this. Instead, I assumed a look of shocked disbelief, and expressed the surprise most people do when they hear that this tropical paradise is without snakes.

He asked me how long my friend and I intended to stay in Honolulu. I told him two days. He asked if I minded if he kept the snakes in his office until we left. He told me to telephone him about an hour before flight time, and he would have someone bring the bag to me so that I could board the plane with my prize. Stunned by the offer, I affected an offhand nonchalance, and told him I thought that would be fine. Amazingly, he asked if the snakes needed food or water, and what he should feed them. I told him that wouldn't be necessary, that they would be all right for two days, but that if he wanted to give them a bowl of water, that would also be fine. And then, incredibly, I walked out of his office.

Kay and I walked out of the airport, rented a car and drove off. We have just paid a short visit to the tropical garden and orchid farm just above where I used to live, not far from here. We're lying on the warm, white sand at Waimea Beach. In the winter, these waters produce twenty-foot waves, and every year tourists are swept away by these immense waves that seem to arise from nowhere. But today, the water is glassy calm, the sun is blessedly warm, and Kay is already asleep beside me.

Kay Harris overlooking Hanauma Bay outside of Honolulu, Hawaii
I think I'll close my eyes, too, just for a minute, submerge any lingering residue of unpleasantness, and focus on the magic that has beguiled me from the very beginning as it continues casting its spell.

About the Author

Michael A. Kroll

Anyone who has lived as long as I have (70+ years) will, like me, have many experiences to fall back on, to tell stories about, and to build on. For me, that includes:

Growing up in the idyllic Ojai Valley, California (where I developed a life-long love of snakes and other reptiles);

Graduating from U.C. Berkeley, where I went to jail (for the first time) as one of nearly 800 students arrested in the 1964 Free Speech Movement;

Joining the Peace Corps, which sent me to Malaysian Borneo to teach English in a Chinese secondary school for three years (and continuing to maintain close relationships with those students 50 years later);

Teaching English as a Second language, among other subjects, in cities across the country;

Seeking to end the death penalty and reform our criminal justice system through direct political activism;

Being asked to inaugurate the national organization, the Death Penalty Information Center in Washington, D.C. as its first Director;

Conducting writing workshops in juvenile halls, jails and prisons, through a program called The Beat Within;

And always writing, writing, writing.

In addition to Beijing and Beyond that chronicles a 1981 tour of China's criminal justice system, I have been published widely in newspapers from The New York Times to the Los Angeles Times, and in publications as disparate as The Nation and Progressive magazines on one hand, and Women's World on the other. Also, in furtherance of my thespian tendencies, I have written two movie scripts (one sold), and a stage play.

Currently, from my home in Oakland, California, I am working on both a mystery novel and a memoir.

AWARDS

1984 Meritorious Achievement Award for Freelance Journalism

Media Alliance, San Francisco

1984 Best Magazine News Feature

Los Angeles Valley Press Club Awarded for "The Fraternity of Death," chronicling the history of the gas chamber in California. It was published in the L.A. Herald Examiner and included in an anthology, *Facing the Death Penalty: Essays on a Cruel and Unusual Punishment,* edited by Michael I. Radelet (1989).

1990 Best Magazine News Feature Western Publishers' Association

Awarded for "Appointment With Death," published in California Lawyer

1990 Eugene Block Journalism Special Recognition Award

Awarded "for work on a universal human rights issue."

<u>Connect with Me</u>

LinkedIn: https://www.linkedin.com/in/michael-kroll-2ab58910/

Website: http://www.michael-a-kroll.com/

Email: michaelkroll@michaelwrites.org

SOME RELEVANT PUBLISHED WORK

By Michael A. Kroll

<u>The Ritual of Executions</u>[1]

The death penalty has become a predictable ritual where all play their expected roles: The D.A., the Defense, the opposing families, the advocates for and against all return to familiar expressions and positions, then all return to resume the lives they led before the execution.

<u>Reliving the Death: Death Penalty's Unintended Consequence</u>[2]

One of the unexplored aspects of a system of capital punishment is its effect on the survivors of murder: family and friends. The process forces them to relive the trauma they experience over and over again, as the capital case goes through its required stages. A punishment of life in prison would eliminate this recurring pain.

<u>Let Life in Prison be the Ultimate Penalty</u>[3]

When the killer of a police officer was not given the death penalty, his family and friends felt like they were cheated because they did not exact the "ultimate penalty." This article argues that such feelings of disrespect can be eliminated by eliminating the death penalty.

<u>Killing Justice: Police Misconduct and the Death Penalty</u>[4]

Misconduct by the government in the pursuit of a death sentence can take many forms. But whether it involves the use of threats and

---

1.   http://news.newamericamedia.org/news/

view_article.html?article_id=7bc4c626c47798753a39b4f7b00dd549

2.   http://news.newamericamedia.org/news/

view_article.html?article_id=907a76c53154b79662bda072690a6d3e

3.   http://news.newamericamedia.org/news/

view_article.html?article_id=7e40c9671527b9626fcef693f66ddbd9

4.   https://deathpenaltyinfo.org/killing-justice

intimidation to obtain a "confession," the use of jailhouse informants who secretly enter into deals with the prosecution for their testimony, or the government's unrevealed promise of leniency for one co-defendant in exchange for his or her testimony against another, the resulting death sentence is fundamentally unfair, and cannot be tolerated in a society which honors the principle that no person is above the law.

<u>Justice on the Cheap: The Philadelphia Story</u>[5]

"Them without the capital get the punishment" is a well-worn phrase among those who have studied the unequal application of the death penalty in America. Poor people facing society's ultimate penalty must rely on public funds to ensure they are competently represented, as the Constitution guarantees. Yet, in more and more jurisdictions, public services of all kinds are being slashed for lack of adequate funding. Philadelphia, Pennsylvania, is one such jurisdiction—a dramatic and graphic example of a nationwide problem.

<u>Chattahoochee Judicial District - the Buckle of the Death Belt: The Death Penalty in Microcosm</u>[6]

Nearly 20 years after the Supreme Court held the death penalty unconstitutional—largely because of racial discrimination—the death penalty in America continues to reflect the worst aspects of our judicial system: racism, unequal treatment of the poor, a shamefully inadequate legal defense system and abuse of discretion by ambitious prosecutors and other politicians seeking higher office. The Chattahoochee Judicial District in Georgia is a microcosm of this national disgrace.

---

5.   https://deathpenaltyinfo.org/justice-on-the-cheap

6.   https://deathpenaltyinfo.org/chattahoochee-judicial-district-buckle-death-belt-death-penalty-microcosm

Read on for a special bonus excerpt from Michael A. Kroll's

soon-to-be-published new mystery novel
Soul of the Matter
Chapter One

It was after two in the a.m. and I was exhausted. As I swung easily into the arching two-lane on-ramp that merges into one before entering the San Francisco Bay Bridge in the far left lane, I expected smooth sailing all the way home to Oakland. The Bay Bridge is one of the architectural wonders of the world. From the upper deck, a diamond necklace of lights rises and falls along both sides, stretched between huge steel towers on intertwining cables as thick as men. The cables are kept from swinging wildly in the powerful wind that sweeps from the Pacific through the Golden Gate by vertical steel strands through which one can see Alcatraz as if through the strings of a giant harp.

I was so dead tired that even the magnificently lit skyline did not revive me. I rolled down my window so the cold wind would rouse me, and was immediately hit with the delicious smell of Hills Brothers coffee brewing just below me where the Bridge overflies the Embarcadero, leaving San Francisco behind.

I wished I had a cup of that coffee right then. Good to the last drop, or was that Maxwell House? I was too tired to care.

Thinking of the sleep that awaited me at home, I was beginning to drowse, dangerously, when I was suddenly aware that brake lights were coming on in front of me. Further ahead, I could see the red glow of slowing cars. My old Datsun clattered to a stop, and I came fully awake, cursing out loud, in my manner.

"Unfriggingbelievable! Shid!"

A traffic jam! At this hour! Traffic wasn't just slowing, it had come to a complete stop. "Looks like a frigging parking lot," I sighed aloud, talking to the universe.

The stillness of the night was shattered by the cacophony of a hundred horns honking up and down the Bridge, as if the driver at the head of the pack had come to a halt merely to take in the view. I rolled the window back up and turned on my car radio, which I leave tuned to the all-night classical station, except when I want to be depressed. Then I listen to the news. The announcer was using his best mortuary voice to introduce Beethoven's 7th Symphony. I put the volume on high in the hopes of drowning out the growing din of automobile horns.

Ah, that first blast of symphonic horns, as much a testament to the creative genius of the human mind as the Bridge itself. Whatever was holding up traffic ahead, it looked like it was going to last awhile, so I tried to let the power of the music carry me to a different place. Instead, I found myself checking out my neighbors.

In my rearview mirror, I watched a kid with nose rings and straw-yellow hair tinged with alfalfa smoking a marijuana cigarette behind the wheel of his maroon BMW with a convertible top. He had flipped on the overhead light, recklessly unafraid of being seen. Next to the BMW was a brown and white Dryer's Ice Cream truck. What with the smell of the coffee still wafting through the air, my three favorite addictions were all represented in that one spot. I drank at least a pot of coffee a day, sometimes more, ate anywhere from a quart to a gallon of ice cream for lunch and dinner–and little else – and lived by the principle that cannabis a day keeps the doctor away. Actually, one ritual joint in the evening, after eating my ice cream dinner. If I smoked before dinner, I could go through all of Baskin-Robbins 31 flavors before getting to dessert.

I thought of getting out of my car, approaching the kid and asking for a hit of his tobacco-less product, but decided against it. The kid would probably think I was hitting on him, and he looked like he was barely sixteen. Anyway, ever since that unfortunate episode in Tennessee, I had vowed never again to smoke in a car, one of the few vows I had actually kept.

A clearly furious Asian woman got out of her car ahead of me. It was one of those cookie-cutter designer cars that all look alike, and I couldn't tell if it was a Toyota or a Taurus, but it was pretty and red and sported a personalized license plate that said LACE.

She stood outside her door with her hand pressing on the horn through the open window, as if her angry impatience would jar loose the logjam. Once, she looked back in my direction as if for encouragement, but I gave none and she turned away, craning her neck to catch sight of whatever disaster lay ahead.

Abreast of me on my right was a beat up old white pick-up truck. On the dented door next to the driver, the words "JJ's Janitorial Service, Soul Proprietor" had been carefully painted in black. That "Soul Proprietor" caught my eye. Soul with a "u." Another example of the declining standards of literacy in the age of e-mail? I had to look up slightly to catch sight of the driver who was calmly speaking to someone on his cell phone, or rather, calmly listening to someone speaking to him on his cell phone.

The Asian woman's horn did not harmonize at all well with Beethoven, so I tried to tune her out. The kid behind me, still puffing away, was either singing or lip synching a rap to judge by the regular punctuation marks he made in the air with his head.

I turned my attention to Soul Proprietor next door. He looked to be in his mid-60s, but had one of those faces Black men sometimes have that make them look younger, even boyish, well into old age. As my eyes accustomed themselves to the dim light, I could see that he had a beautiful head of snow white hair, and I mentally added ten years to the age I had given him.

There was something about this man that pulled me in. I never saw him utter more than one word at a time to his phone partner, nor did

I see any indication that anything was registering on that smooth face of his. He gave no token of what he was thinking or feeling if, indeed, he was thinking or feeling anything. And then, slowly, he glanced down toward me. Our eyes met just as the second movement of the magnificent 7th began its slow dirge.

I cannot describe the effect his eyes had on me. It was not merely the dark emotions conjured by the music that brought me to the brink of tears. It was him. It was those eyes that looked through me, beyond me to some distant place that only he could see. It was as if he, too, were listening to the grief-stricken lament of the music rather than to some disembodied voice on a cell phone. There was such pain in his eyes, such sadness, and something else I could not quite identify. Anger? Fear?

"Fear." I said the word out loud and realized that it was I who was afraid. Afraid of what? Those eyes just kept looking at me without seeing, as if trying to understand what he was hearing. I smiled as warmly as I could, but his expression did not change, did not acknowledge my existence.

I shivered, and turned away. Fog was now pouring over the railing and onto the Bridge like special effects in some dream sequence in a Hollywood extravaganza. "Little cat's feet my arse," I heard myself say. It was more like a sudden, silent tide, cold as an anaconda.

The somber cellos kept beating out their dark, rhythmic tattoo as Beethoven's funereal strains moved towards their conclusion.

I shivered again, and turned back to Soul Proprietor. Still holding the phone, he was climbing out of his pick-up and into the fog. Now he looked at me dead on, and his eyes seemed huge, as if he had taken LSD. But unlike the wild, vague stare of an acid head, JJ's huge eyes were now totally focused on mine. Our eyes were locked together, synchronized, and our heads swiveled in slow motion as he made his way between LACE, blaring her horn ahead of me, and my own car.

I reached up and locked the door. In return, he flashed me a menacing look that caused me to shiver again. He stopped and cocked his head slightly. A barely perceptible smile gave his face a quizzical look, as if to say, "Do you believe a simple lock can keep me from you?" I thought I saw him shake his head once, but it was too small a movement to be sure it wasn't just an involuntary tic.

And then he was walking again. Time seemed to slow down. I glanced in the mirror at the boy in the BMW behind me who was now watching us. Would he gallantly leap from his car and save me? Did I need saving?

I am not the kind of man who puts much stock in visions or ESP, or that sort of thing, but suddenly I had a premonition that death was near. Had I triggered something murderous in his demented head by locking my door? Was that mechanical act of self-protection his final indignity, one locked door too many?

The straw-haired boy toked deeply on what was left of his joint, and I squeezed my eyes shut and inhaled simultaneously, breathing in the coffee-flavored tangy salt air. My heart was pounding. I opened my eyes, and once more turned my gaze on JJ – just in time to see Soul Proprietor put his right hand on the railing, his left still clutching his phone, look at me with such contempt I could not fathom its depth, and vault over the side of the Bridge.

****

For information about how to purchase Soul of the Matter when it is published,
published,
please contact Michael at:
Website: http://www.michael-a-kroll.com/
Email: michaelkroll@michaelwrites.org